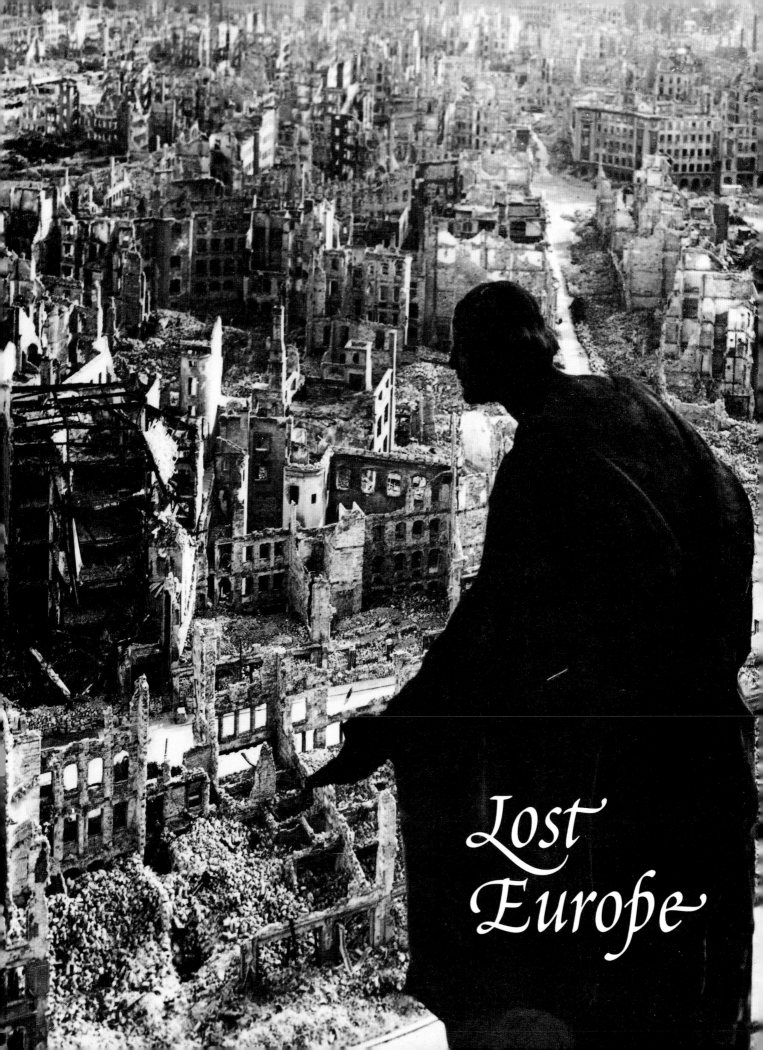

Lost
Europe

Lost Europe

IMAGES OF A VANISHED WORLD

Jean Loussier &
Robin Langley Sommer, EDITORS

Grange
BOOKS

Page 1 photograph:
Dresden, Germany, at the end of World War II.

Pages 2–3 photograph:
Leeuwarden, the Netherlands. The picturesque canalside scene in this 1940s photograph of 't Vliet has vanished: the waterside buildings were demolished and the canal filled in for a traffic-improvement scheme.

For

Maureen,

Keith, Linda,

Kate, Rachel

and John

THE CONTRIBUTORS

Jean Loussier was born in Lyons, France, and grew up in Scotland. He studied history at the University of Oxford, and worked for many years as a translator, writer and editor specialising in history and the arts before retiring to western Scotland. He now divides his time between his two passions: history and the natural environment.

Robin Langley Sommer is a freelance writer and editor whose numerous works on architecture and the decorative arts include *Frank Lloyd Wright* (1992), *The Arts and Crafts Movement* (1995), *American Architecture: An Illustrated History* (1996) and *The Old Barn Book* (1997).

Keith Hunt studied architecture and town planning at Manchester University. After gaining experience in town centre design and housing redevelopment at Lancashire County Council, he entered private practice. During twenty-seven years as a principal, he undertook projects including schools, university buildings, hospitals, housing, churches and industrial development as well as town centre redevelopment. He retired in 1991 and is now a town-planning consultant with a special interest in conservation and the rehabilitation of urban centres.

Jos Smit studied architectural history at the University of Amsterdam. He is co-author of *Dutch Building Design, A History of Ten Centuries of Architecture* (1995), as well as *The Canal Book* (1991), its successor volume, *The Canal Book II* (1992), and *Amsterdam, Monuments and Windmills* (1994). He is the editor of *De Sluitsteen*, a magazine on nineteenth- and twentieth-century architecture and applied arts.

Anke van Zanten grew up in Ghent, Belgium, during World War II. She teaches modern European history in Brussels and is active in restoration and conservation projects.

Clara Brenger was born in Cologne in 1953. She studied art history and urban conservation at the Universität zu Köln, as well as the history of architecture, city planning and urban design at Stuttgart University. Now an architectural consultant, her special interests include Expressionist architecture and the Bauhaus.

Mila Riggio is a freelance writer and architectural historian who grew up in Italy and England. The author of numerous articles on Gothic architecture, she gained a degree in medieval history from London University and has since studied in Florence and Naples.

Danielle Sremac was born in Belgrade, Yugoslavia, and moved to the United States in 1976. She received a Master's Degree in International Affairs at the American University School of International Service in Washington, D.C., and has worked as a consultant on trade with Central and Eastern Europe and an economic analyst at the U.S. Department of Agriculture. Since 1992 Ms. Sremac has been a consultant on public relations and international affairs, and a representative of Serbian-Americans in Washington, D.C., as president of the Serbian American Council. Ms. Sremac advises non-governmental and governmental institutions in former Yugoslavia. She has written extensively on the Balkan crisis and addressed numerous international affairs institutes in the United States and elsewhere. She is currently writing a book entitled *Serbian Chronicle: Struggle Against a War of Words and Bullets.*

Istvan Lazarescu teaches modern history and is active in environmental issues in California, where he has lived since leaving his native Romania.

Vasile Toch, who consulted and researched photographs for the Romanian section of this book, is an emigré Romanian architect and sculptor who works with his wife and partner, Susan Norrie, near Edinburgh, Scotland. In 1995 he sponsored "Lost Bucharest," an exhibition on lost Romanian buildings with the Romanian Cultural Attaché in Edinburgh.

Jim Curtis, Professor of Russian at the University of Missouri-Columbia, received his BA in German from Vanderbilt University, and his Ph.D. in Russian from Columbia University in 1968. He is the author of three books, including *Solzhenitsyn's Traditional Imagination*, and numerous articles and book reviews. In 1994 he was co-director of an NEH Summer Institute, "Moscow: Architecture and Art in Historical Context."

Project Editor: Sara Hunt
Editors: Jean Loussier and Robin Langley Sommer
Art Director: Charles J. Ziga
Photo Research: Amanda Little
Research: Elaine Lonergan

Published by Grange Books
An Imprint of Grange Books PLC
The Grange
Grange Yard
London SE1 3AG

This edition published 1997

Copyright © 1997 Saraband Inc.

Design © Ziga Design

ISBN: 1-85627-863-8

Printed in China

10 9 8 7 6 5 4 3 2 1

Contents

Introduction

The twentieth century has brought incalculable changes to the world that existed in 1900, some of them beneficial, like the advances in medicine and natural science, others traumatic and destructive, including warfare on a global scale with weapons lethal to both humankind and the environment. The process that social scientist Alvin Toffler named "future shock" has affected whole generations, as familiar folkways, values, communities, occupations and landmarks are challenged or eradicated by new technology, beliefs and cultural icons.

Europe, where Western civilisation took form over three millennia, has played a major role in effecting the changes of modern times and has been, in turn, deeply affected by them. National boundaries have been drawn and redrawn by war and revolution. Ethnic and cultural demarcations have been blurred. Entire ethnic and religious groups have been targeted for genocide, as in Nazi Germany and former Yugoslavia. The attrition of religious belief has emptied many churches in some countries, while in others, like Poland and Hungary, sustained persecution by occupying powers and totalitarian régimes failed to destroy the spiritual heritage of the people despite the destruction or secularisation of their churches and synagogues.

The sweeping changes of the century have affected the manmade landscape of Europe — its architecture — in many ways. Apart from the loss of beautiful and historic buildings to war and civil unrest, comparable losses have been deliberately incurred by narrow views that define progress as "out with the old, in with the new." Rapid commercial development has been allowed to override considerations of historic preservation in many parts of the United Kingdom, Italy, France, Belgium, the Netherlands, Germany and other western European nations — although most of these countries have developed increased awareness of their architectural heritage as the century progressed. Likewise, national and local government attempts to improve infrastructure and modernise industry to maintain economic competitiveness have resulted in the loss of landmark bridges, waterfronts, canals and residential sections dating back to the Middle Ages, as well as blighting the natural landscape. Until it was finally stopped in 1989, the unprecedented destruction imposed by the Romanian government in the name of social engineering razed entire sections of Bucharest, numerous towns and villages and such irreplaceable monuments as the Vacaresti Monastery and Suceava's medieval city centre. Stalin's regime visited widespread destruction on magnificent religious architecture and other "bourgeois" landmarks to further his ideological cause in the years 1928–53.

Natural disasters, including floods, fires and earthquakes, have also taken their toll of Europe's architectural heritage. In 1908 an earthquake that claimed 83,000 lives destroyed the ancient Sicilian city of Messina, established as a Greek colony about 500 BC and ceded to Rome after the First Punic War. It was later rebuilt as a modern city. Skopje, Macedonia (former Yugoslavia), capital of the Serbian kingdom during the 1200s, was levelled by an earthquake in 1963, leaving half its residents homeless and almost 2,000 dead. Flooding in Florence, Italy, in 1966 damaged many works of art, books and museum collections: an international effort to restore these works was undertaken to good effect. Saragossa, Spain, a former Roman colony that served as capital for the kingdom of Aragon suffered a destructive fire in 1979 and central Romania was flooded in 1970. The earthquake that followed seven years later did major damage in and around Bucharest and served as the pretext for additional demolition by government planners.

Given the vast extent of architectural changes and losses incurred in Europe over the past century, a comprehensive record of lost architecture would fill many volumes: we have, of necessity, chosen for this book only a few examples from a limited number of countries. Our survey features chapters on countries that have suffered major losses of their traditional architecture, which, taken together, illustrate the various processes involved. Countries whose pace of change has been slower and less extreme than that of their neighbours, including Ireland and the Scandinavian states, are not explored in this overview. Also excluded are Portugal, Spain and Greece, where modern commercial development of coastal areas for tourism has resulted in dramatic changes to the natural landscape, while the architectural heritage of their historic cities, towns and villages remains, for the most part, little affected.

While our selection of countries, and the contributors' selections of individual cities and buildings, can document only a fraction of the changes, the study reveals a remarkable fact: the extent of architectural losses is almost equally great in countries where the causes of change differ dramatically. The deliberate destruction ordered by dictators like Stalin and Ceausescu is mirrored in the extensive architectural casualties of many western European nations, due to their drive for modernisation and progress and the underregulation of construction by private enterprise. It is fair to say that wartime raids, ethnic offensives, occupying dictatorships and totalitarian régimes have targeted particular landmarks—mainly religious buildings and monuments—while non-ideologically planned demolition has, in the main, spared such historic treasures. But a closer look reveals that many important structures in western Europe have disappeared at the hands of planners and developers despite their cultural and architectural significance.

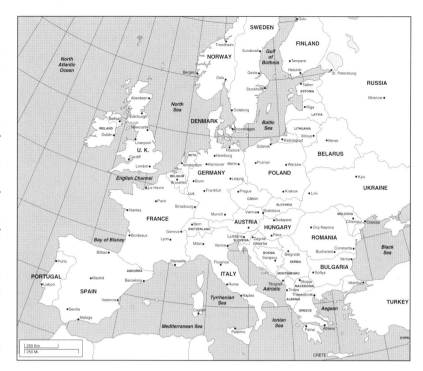

Unlike other art forms, which are generally in the hands of museums and private collectors, architecture, with its attendant sculpture, carving, frescoes, murals and mosaics, is a communal link with a people's history and cultural heritage. It is a highly visible and deeply felt bond, engendering a sense of pride and continuity with one's ethnic, spiritual and national origins. In his introduction to *Lost Treasures of Europe* (Pantheon Books, 1946), Ernest T. DeWald, who worked with Allied and indigenous forces to protect monuments, works of art and archives during World War II, tells a story that illustrates this point: "When, late in the spring of 1945, the famous bronze equestrian statue of Cosimo de' Medici by Gian da Bologna was returned to Florence from its temporary hiding place…a Florentine cabby, who happened to be crossing the Piazza della Signoria as the truck bearing the statue was entering the piazza, stood up in his cab, snapped his whip, and shouted at the top of his lungs: *'Ben tornato, Cosimo!'* (Welcome home, Cosimo!)."

The former landmarks described here— whether palaces, industrial and civic structures or simply dwellings typical of local traditions—include those of the United Kingdom, France, the Netherlands, Belgium, Germany, Italy, Romania, Russia and the

Above: Old Market Square in Warsaw, Poland, prior to World War II. Warsaw's old city centre was destroyed in the war, but much of it—including the square—was rebuilt.

republics of former Yugoslavia. Chapter introductions have been provided by architects, conservationists and historians with considerable local knowledge—most of them natives of the countries described. Each offers an informed and personal inside view that throws additional light upon the illustrations they have helped to select for this volume. Their individual special interests have led them to focus on widely differing aspects of the many causes of architectural change, but the overall picture they portray provides a unique and fascinating overview.

In the British Isles, the loss of cultural monuments over the past hundred years has resulted from several factors, including urbanisation, warfare, dereliction and neglect and, especially during the 1960s, overly zealous commercial development and efforts to improve the infrastructure of major cities with insufficient regard to conservation. In London, historic commercial and residential districts (only a small proportion of which had suffered damage during the Blitz) were pulled down to make room for faceless skyscrapers and retail complexes that are at variance with the city's rich and diverse architectural heritage. The commercial port of Liverpool, on the River Mersey in northwestern England, which had the first wet dock in Great Britain (1709), is a shipping and rail centre whose historical importance as a conduit for trade is second only to London's.

Seven miles of thriving docks were gradually diminished by decades of economic and industrial change, until "modernisation" was inevitable. Village churches in the sturdy Norman style—some 7,000 were built in the century following the Norman Conquest of 1066—fell into disrepair as their congregations shrank, due to urbanisation and secularisation. Historic country houses were demolished or converted to other uses, as social change made it impossible for owners to maintain large estates.

Although Great Britain never recovered its status as a pre-eminent world power after the losses it sustained in World War I, the most devastating physical damage was inflicted by German bombing raids during World War II. The catalogue of buildings, even several towns, destroyed is a long one, and subsequent reconstruction has not entirely restored either physical or cultural damage.

The precincts of Canterbury Cathedral, a place of pilgrimage since the death of Thomas à Becket in 1170, were severely damaged and partially destroyed. In Plymouth, St. Andrew's Church, a fifteenth-century Gothic landmark with a continuous barrel roof and carved granite capitals and shafts, was bombed and burned to a shell. Exeter suffered heavy damage to its twelfth-century cathedral and demolition of Tudor town houses dating from the sixteenth century, with their overhanging upper stories and leaded casement windows. The resort of Bath, whose classical architecture was inspired in part by the city's associations with ancient Rome, was a study in style and symmetry. Its extensive Royal Crescent, a monument to eighteenth-century English architecture, was heavily damaged.

In Coventry, widespread destruction claimed St. Michael's Cathedral, a splendid example of the perpendicular Gothic style of the fourteenth century; the guild meeting place, St. Mary's Hall, which was famous for its eighteenth-century tapestries; and Ford's Hospital, a unique half-timbered building dating from the early 1500s. Nearby Birmingham was also hard hit. However, the greatest number of losses occurred in London, including Chelsea Old Church, where St. Thomas More worshipped in the early 1500s; All Hallows, Barking, a blend of Norman and Gothic elements; St. Brides, rebuilt from an old church by Christopher Wren in 1670–84; the fifteenth-century Guild Hall; portions of the four great Inns of Court; Merchant Taylors' Hall; and Portman House, whose interior was a masterwork of the eighteenth-century architect Robert Adams.

In Ireland, destruction preceded and followed the Home Rule Act of 1920, which divided the country into two parts: twenty-six southern counties loyal to the Sinn Fein independence movement and six loyalist counties in the north, shaped from the Ulster area. The Anglo-Irish war continued for another year after the southern counties rejected Home Rule. Architectural casualties of the Sinn Fein rioting included Dublin's Old Post Office in Sackville Street. Many other structures have since suffered in the ongoing struggle between the Irish Republican Army, outlawed in 1974 as a result of terrorist acts, and the British government.

Across the channel from the British Isles, France suffered severe damage in both World Wars: much of the fighting in western Europe was waged on her soil. During World War I, the ancient fortress town of Verdun, facing the German frontier, was the focal point of the longest battle in history, in which a million combatants were killed. Also destroyed were the town's beautiful twelfth-century cathedral, a Benedictine abbey dating from the ninth century, the seventeenth-century town hall and virtually every dwelling. Additional damage was sustained in the former French province of Alsace, ceded to Germany in 1871 but recovered by France in 1919 through the Treaty of Versailles. The ancient northern city of Arras, with its Gothic cathedral, 245-foot belfry built by the medieval townspeople, and richly ornamented Hotel de Ville, was almost entirely destroyed.

France experienced even greater losses during World War II, not from the German occupation, but from the Allied invasion of Europe through Normandy. The Channel ports,

including St. Malo and Calais, were particularly hard hit. At Calais, the Porte de Guise, a remnant of the Wool Market built here by the English in the early sixteenth century, was destroyed, and the old City Hall, with its octagonal Renaissance steeple and massive free-standing belfry, were heavily damaged. The city of Rouen, an episcopal seat since the third century and the capital of Normandy from 912, lost part of its thirteenth-century cathedral, the Palais de Justice (Law Courts), the small Gothic church of Saint-Vincent (apart from the stained-glass windows, which had been removed) and many other medieval structures between the cathedral and the Seine. At Lisieux, characteristic Renaissance houses with richly carved structural members were largely destroyed, as was the Church of Saint-Jacques, a fine example of the flamboyant Gothic style completed in 1501. Other French cities that suffered substantial damage include Vendôme, Nevers, Chartres and Marseilles.

The natural disasters that took their toll of Italian monuments during the twentieth century have already been mentioned. The country has three active volcanoes—Mounts Vesuvius, Etna and Stromboli—and the forces that produce them also cause frequent earthquakes. The Po River brings the threat of severe floods when the Alpine snows melt every spring, and engineers have built dikes to protect northern Italy since the time of Leonardo da Vinci. Italy's volatile political life has seen several important cities, including Trieste and Fiume, change hands repeatedly, and Mussolini's dictatorship (1922-45) not only destroyed portions of ancient Rome and many other old cities in the name of urban renewal, but led the nation into World War II on the Axis side. The destruction that accompanied the Allied invasion of southern Italy, Rome and German-held northern Italy during the last two years of the war is a sad litany of cultural treasures lost. It includes the Benedictine abbey of Monte Cassino, founded in 529; the Baroque church of Santa Chiara in Naples, originally a Norman structure; several Florentine monuments, including the incomparable Ponte Santa Trinita, a Renaissance

Above: The quiet village of Marbella, Spain, before it became the most fashionable Mediterranean resort outside the French Riviera.

bridge across the Arno (since restored); Pisa's Gothic Medici Palace and Camposanto; the elegant seventeenth-century Farnese Theatre in Parma; and Milan's Marino and Royal Palaces. Still greater losses would have been incurred if not for Allied activities under the auspices of Monuments, Fine Arts and Archives commissions. Extensive restoration was undertaken after World War II in cases where masonry walls and façades survived, but as Ernest DeWald observed in 1946, "no resuscitating power can ever bring back the frescoes of Mantegna in Padua or those of Melozzo at Forli."

The Netherlands, bordering on Germany, Belgium and the North Sea, has a coastline deeply indented by the mouths of the Rhine and Scheldt and by the Zuider Zee, a reclamation project undertaken in 1918. Originally a lake in the middle of a large swampland, it had become an ocean gulf as a result of flooding during the early Middle Ages. This arm of the North Sea penetrated into the southern coast of the Netherlands. Reclamation began with construction of a dike between the Zuider Zee and the ocean; after decades of work, the area was drained and became an important resort, while the extensive system of dikes added some 550,000 acres of arable land to the nation.

The Netherlands became a great maritime power during the seventeenth century, with the formation of the Dutch East India Company. Amsterdam and Rotterdam were, and are, the major centres of commerce. Important cultural centres dating from the twelfth and thirteenth centuries include Middleburg, Arnhem, Venlo and Heusden. Nijmegen, founded by the Romans, is the nation's oldest town.

During World War I, the Netherlands maintained neutrality, but the country and its people suffered great depredation during World War II. Germany attacked without warning on May 10, 1940, and occupied the country after bombarding the great port of Rotterdam. The old section of the city was levelled and the *Groote Kerk*, or Church of St. Lawrence, a Gothic structure begun in 1412, was largely ruined. The old city of Maastricht, where building stone was quarried, served as a center for Dutch resistance fighters throughout the five-year German occupation.

Important buildings were lost at Middelburg, including the eighteenth-century Military Hospital, formerly a guild hall; the Abbey of St. Nicholas, founded in 1128 by monks from Antwerp; and the late Gothic Town Hall, which was restored after the war. Beautiful Arnhem, residence of the dukes of Guelders (1233–1538), was heavily damaged.

It took heroic effort for the Dutch people to rebuild their shattered economy and their infrastructure after the war, but this was largely accomplished before 1960. Since that time, unfortunately, the wrecker's ball has razed many historic waterfronts, windmills, residences and elegant old resorts in the name of modernisation.

Belgium, independent from the neighbouring Netherlands since 1832, was a prosperous industrialised country in 1900, famous for its diamond industry, centred in Antwerp, and the lace made at Brussels and Bruges. Historic universities flourished at Ghent, Liège, Brussels and Louvain, and privileges secured by the industrious burghers of the old towns were long protected by the constitutional monarchy.

The invasion and occupation of Belgium by Germany during World War I struck a crippling blow to industry: engines, equipment and material were shipped to Germany, and thousands of workmen were deported there. However, far greater physical destruction was visited upon Belgium during World War II, beginning with the surprise attack of May 10, 1940, when the Germans reoccupied the country. Fierce fighting throughout the war left its mark in Hoogstraten, where the stone-and-brick Gothic Town Hall and the Gothic Church of St. Catherine were demolished; and in Nivelles, where the eleventh-century convent Church of St. Gertrude was severely damaged. Its reliquary, an unsurpassed example of Flemish Gothic goldwork, was destroyed.

Louvain's fourteenth-century church of St. Gertrude, with Gothic choir stalls carved by Mathias de Wayer of Brussels about 1550, was another casualty of the conflict, as was St. Peter's Church at Bastogne, focal point of the 1944 Battle of the Bulge. Hardest hit was Tournai, a city rich in architectural monuments including Romanesque, Gothic, Medieval and Renaissance. Whole sections of the old town were destroyed, including graceful mansions in the style of Louis XIV, who conquered the city in 1667.

The aggressive policies of German rulers from Kaiser Wilhelm II to Adolf Hitler had devastating effects on their country during the twentieth century. The kaiser's imperialistic ambitions had divided Europe into two camps—pro- and anti-German—by the time World War I broke out in 1914. Huge territories conquered and annexed during the nineteenth century were lost when Germany was overcome by the Triple Entente of Britain, France and Russia during the four-year struggle.

A bitter and disaffected Germany was susceptible to the blandishments of Hitler, who came to power in 1933 as chancellor of the shaky Weimar Republic. By 1939 he had violated the 1919 Treaty of Versailles by rearming Germany, annexing Austria and part of Czechoslovakia and attacking Poland to "recover" the Free City of Danzig. The latter action finally precipitated a declaration of war by Britain and France, who were bound

by treaty to protect Poland. In the interim, the medieval city of Danzig, a great power in the Hanseatic League, was almost destroyed, and Warsaw suffered devastating losses, including its Old Market Square; the Polish Baroque Krasinski Palace; and Castle (Sigismund) Square, with its seventeenth-century royal residence, including the magnificent Hall of Audiences added in the late eighteenth century along with the Ball Room designed by Domenico Merlini. Most of Warsaw's war damage has since been meticulously restored.

The destruction wrought in Poland would be replicated in Germany many times over, especially after the Soviet Union joined the Allies in 1941. Continuous aerial assault levelled large sections of ancient Cologne, including St. Maria im Kapitol, consecrated in 1649; the thirteenth-century Church of St. Andrew and its environs; the medieval City Hall with its Renaissance porch; and the twelfth-century church dedicated to St. Ursula and her companions. Frankfurt-am-Main suffered extensive damage, as did Münster, Mainz and Trier. Stuttgart lost its historic Church of the Holy Cross, the Old Palace (1553) and the New Palace, built for Duke Karl Eugen after 1744 in the Baroque style of Versailles. Nuremberg, one of Europe's great medieval cities, suffered heavy damages, and the elegant city of Dresden was almost completely destroyed. Munich's *Residenz* of the dukes of Bavaria,

Above: *Rockingham House, Co. Roscommon, Ireland: a three-storey Classical mansion that was partially destroyed by fire in 1957 and subsequently demolished.*

including one of the world's earliest museums, was largely ruined, along with the old marketplace, the *Marienplatz,* and several historic churches. The damage to Berlin, where the warring factions converged in 1945 and Hitler committed suicide, was very great. Before it was partitioned by the victorious Allies, many cultural monuments were in ruins. They included the Charlottenberg Schloß, a summer residence in the Baroque style crowned by a cupola tower; the *Französische Kirche* and the *Neue Kirche,* with classical additions commissioned by Frederick the Great; the Roman Baroque *schloss* built for the kings of Prussia by Andreas Schlüter beginning in 1698 and *Monbijou,* which housed the Hohenzollern Museum.

Extensive reconstruction and new building have taken place in Germany, reunified after decades of partition, and the people's attachment to their cultural monuments and strong sense of history have ensured sensitive restoration wherever possible. Despite the rise of contemporary buildings with the renewal of German prosperity, the conservation movement protecting historic structures is strong.

In central Europe, Austria was subjected to air raids and several historic buildings in Vienna, notably the upper Belvedere (1721–3) and *Stephansdom,* a late Gothic hall-form church, were damaged. Additional destruction took place during the Soviet occupation. Hungary suffered even greater losses after the war, when it became a Communist satellite country.

The Balkan peninsula, historically an agricultural and pastoral region, has experienced sporadic conflict throughout the twentieth century, with attendant destruction of its folkways and cultural heritage. The Greeks and the Albanians are the longest-established ethnic groups in this region. Successive waves of invasion or migration brought the Romans, Slavs, Bulgarians, Magyars and Turks. The Turkish power, dominant from 1453, was broken in the Balkan Wars (1912–13), while the spirit of nationalism, which had grown in strength throughout the latter half of the nineteenth century, resulted after World War I

in the creation of independent states along ethnographical lines. This book focuses on two of those entities whose architectural losses have been especially heavy during the twentieth century: Romania and the republics of former Yugoslavia.

The Romanians descend from an amalgamation of the earlier inhabitants of Dacia with Roman colonists. During World War I, the nation joined the Allies (1916) and was immediately occupied by the Central Powers for her wheat and oil fields. However, advantageous treaties with Austria, Hungary and Bulgaria in 1919 restored all that had been lost and more than doubled her area and population, adding to the country's minorities, concentrated in the west. The influence of these minorities, including Hungarians, Germans, Ukrainians and Yugoslavs, is apparent in Romania's rich and diverse cultural heritage, which was most severely attacked, not during the World War II occupation by the Germans, but by the nation's own Communist government, which took power in 1947. It broke with Soviet Russia in 1964 and moved toward dictatorship with the accession of Nicolae Ceausescu.

Subsequently, the régime implemented the Urban and Rural Systemisation Law of 1974, which opened the way for wholesale demolition of towns and villages. The nation's agricultural workers were to be resettled from their private homes and gardens into high-rise tenements in new "agro-industrial" complexes. Bucharest, the capital, and other important cities, including Cluj, in Transylvania, Timisoara, Chisinau and Cernauti, were to be modernised—a euphemism for the destruction of innumerable historic churches, civic centres, neighbourhoods and fortifications dating from the Middle Ages. This process was facilitated by the major earthquake that struck near Bucharest in 1977, which damaged many buildings and furnished the rationale for destroying others, and by the dissolution of the nation's vigilant Directorate for Historic Monuments (1977). Within a dozen years, some twenty-nine towns had been razed and rebuilt in "collectivist" style, obliterating old streets and avenues along with the private dwellings. The heart of central Bucharest, once one of Europe's most beautiful cities, had been levelled, with the relocation or destruction of such cultural treasures as the Eastern Orthodox Vacaresti monastery (1716–22) and the Mihai Voda monastery. Mansions, villas, private houses and apartment buildings and the landmark known as Uranus Hill, an area filled with characteristic Romanian art and architecture, all disappeared. Entire blocks were bulldozed. Comparable destruction was going on in the countryside, where some 8,000 villages of the country's 13,000 had been scheduled for destruction by the year 2000.

Fortunately, this massive experiment in social engineering was halted in 1989, when the oppressive Ceausescu regime was overthrown by a popular revolution. Romania still faced major problems of poverty and displacement, but a considerable part of its urban and cultural heritage had been spared, despite the heavy losses of the 1970s and '80s.

Cataclysmic changes had occurred in Russia during the nineteenth century, and they continued throughout the twentieth. At the turn of the century, Russia had only recently been propelled from the Middle Ages into modern times by the freeing of the serfs, in 1861. The Romanov tsar Nicholas II, who ruled from 1894 until the Revolution of 1917, tried to appease the land hunger of the peasantry and his liberal critics, including the Marxists and other intellectuals, with halfhearted measures that satisfied no one. Russia's entry into World War I, in hope of extending her influence over the Slavic peoples of the Balkans and gaining territory there, came to grief on the battlefield and in the capital, St. Petersburg, where Bolshevik troops attacked the Winter Palace and took control of the government in October 1917. From this point, Russian culture as it had been known began to disintegrate — or, at least, go "underground." A bloody civil war ensued, until Lenin, having moved the seat of government to Moscow in 1918, founded the Union of Soviet Socialist Republics in 1922.

Among the first targets of destruction were the many landed estates that had grown up since the foundation of the Romanov dynasty in 1613. Their gracious manor houses, as described in the novels of Leo Tolstoy, were pulled down or burned as collectivisation swept European Russia. The monuments of the Russian Orthodox Church, influenced by the Byzantine style imported to Kievan Russia before the Mongol Conquest of 1240, fell into disrepair and neglect as the Communist régime suppressed religious observance, especially during the Stalin years. Most damaging of all was the Soviet Union's participation in World War II, which cost millions of lives and additional fragmentation of the country's cultural heritage.

At the beautiful city of Novgorod, founded in the ninth century, the medieval Kremlin, a stone square encircled by walls and towers, was partially destroyed, and the Spas Nereditsky Church (Church of the Transfiguration), dating from 1198, was demolished. The church had been adorned with fresco paintings in the ancient Russian style and with a Byzantine mosaic, the Orante Madonna. At Istra, the Voskrensky Monastery, founded by Patriarch Nicon in 1658, was totally destroyed. In St. Petersburg (whose Russified name was Petrograd, renamed Leningrad upon Lenin's death in 1924), the Winter Palace designed for Elizabeth Petrovna by Rastrelli in the mid-1700s was severely damaged but eventually restored.

The Great Palace at Peterhof, designed for Peter the Great in imitation of Versailles by J.-B. Leblond (1715), with additions in the Russian style by Empress Elizabeth, was ruined. So was the Alexander Palace at Dyetskoye-Selo, built by Catherine the Great for her grandson, the future Tsar Alexander I. Built by Giacomo Quarenghi during the 1790s, it was an imposing structure in the Roman revival mode. Another monument to Alexander's reign is the Admiralty in St. Petersburg, damaged but since restored.

The German origins of Catherine the Great were one of several influences apparent in the magnificent Catherine Palace, built at

Above: *The beautiful Elisabet Bridge over the Danube in Budapest before it was destroyed by the German army of occupation in 1944. All the city's bridges were blown up to block the Soviet advance, but most were rebuilt after the war.*

Dyetskoye-Selo by Empress Elizabeth to designs by Rastrelli. This Baroque complex combined German, Italian and Russian elements in a lavish mélange of color and form enriched by materials imported from many parts of the world at staggering expense.

After the war, many landmarks in Moscow were demolished by the government in the name of progress, including the Monastery of the Passion, founded in 1641 by Tsar Mikhail Fyodorov, and much of the Arbat area, razed to create the modern, mile-long Kallinin Prospect during the 1960s. However, the oldest section of the city, built on a concentric pattern with the Kremlin at its heart, was largely spared reconstruction.

On the Balkan peninsula, the amalgamation of ancient and ethnically diverse kingdoms into the nation called Yugoslavia, "Kingdom of Serbs, Croats and Slovenes," in 1917 did little to resolve the long-standing rivalries that had fragmented the region repeatedly since the sixth century AD. The

country was racked by civil war during World War II and reorganized under Marshal Josip Broz Tito in 1945 into six republics: Serbia, Croatia, Bosnia-Hercegovina, Macedonia, Slovenia and Montenegro.

The Yugoslav capital of Belgrade, Serbia, suffered extensive damage during World Wars I and II, but considerable renovation was carried out during the postwar years. Zagreb, the capital of Croatia, was spared most of this destruction: it has evolved more naturally into a modern section along the River Sava and the older city on the surrounding hills. Ljubljana, Slovenia's capital city, also survived these conflicts relatively unscathed. The most destructive event in the region in modern times was, of course, the civil war of the 1990s, which damaged the historic Croatian city of Dubrovnik to some degree but almost destroyed entire cities and towns in Bosnia-Hercegovina, including Sarajevo, Mostar and Banja Luka. The best-known casualty of the war is Mostar's Stari Most bridge over the

Neretva River *(cover)*, dating from the Ottoman Empire. Many other monuments, churches, mosques and civic centres were also destroyed or damaged. While the incalculable human suffering inflicted by the warring parties on their civilians overshadows the issue of architectural loss, the physical scars borne by these cities serve as a constant, ghastly reminder of the war.

In 1877 William Morris, the visionary English artist who founded the Arts and Crafts Movement, established the Society for the Preservation of Ancient Buildings. Morris and his colleagues did much to raise public awareness of the damaging environmental effects of unbridled growth and industrialisation, emphasising that the abundance of "old buildings" and natural resources previously taken for granted was finite and diminishing. By the turn of the century, the need for preservation—a relatively new concept—was becoming accepted.

It is important to remember that conservation and restoration are not merely a function of salvaging historic buildings that have been damaged by natural or manmade disasters, and that the issues that must be addressed are often complex. Over the past thirty years or so, public awareness of the value of our architectural heritage has increased, along with concern for the natural environment. As populations continue to rise—with attendant problems including traffic congestion—and space in our cities and towns becomes ever-more pressured, more creative solutions are constantly required to balance conflicting land-use needs without destroying buildings of value or the character of residential communities. Meanwhile, architectural conservationists have broadened their scope to include the landmark buildings of the twentieth century, like those of Victor Horta and Erich Mendelsohn featured in this book, that were demolished before their aesthetic merit was recognised. It is also increasingly felt that the safeguarding of a single landmark building is not necessarily a success in conservation terms if its surroundings are not preserved:

accordingly, whole areas are now being identified as worthy of protection or restoration.

Perhaps the most exciting such project of recent times is the faithful recreation of Shakespeare's Globe Theatre in Bankside, a stretch of the south bank of London's River Thames, as the centre of an educational complex that also includes the Inigo Jones Theatre. While it would be impossible to recreate the Elizabethan-era Bankside district—a veritable warren of thatched wooden structures (thatch was banned as early as 1212 in London, and the ban was enforced after the 1666 Fire of London)—every conceivable effort has been made to promote awareness of the Shakespearean environment. Known as the "Wooden 'O'," the circular Globe, an open-air theatre-in-the-round, has been reconstructed from period sketches and descriptions, and built of materials and techniques considered historically accurate (with concealed modifications for safety purposes). Initially the ambitious dream of American actor Sam Wanamaker as early as 1949, the Globe project became "a story with one towering hero and a supporting cast of thousands," according to its official historian, Barry Day; it opened to audiences in 1997.

The question of how to protect our natural resources while moving forward with the times is one of the greatest challenges of our day: it is being debated in each town and country of the globe, and it is also a pressing international issue for our "global village." Through the concerted efforts of local conservationists, municipalities, national governments and art historians, great strides have been made toward elevating our cultural heritage to a similarly high priority, preserving the best of the past *before* it falls into disrepair or succumbs to the bulldozers of commerce and modernisation. The editors of this volume hope that it will contribute to the growing consensus that the manmade landscape forms a vital part of each nation's cultural patrimony and should be treated as a social and spiritual resource of inestimable value.

—Robin Langley and Jean Loussier

The United Kingdom

It is a perennial feature of the man-built world that notable or typical buildings have been lost to posterity for a wide variety of reasons. Britain is no exception. The early shelters of primitive man disappeared largely through the impermanence of their construction, except where they were adaptations of caves. Man has a better record of perpetuating his constructions in monuments to the dead or to the gods—such structures as the Great Pyramids, ziggurats, temples and stone circles. Resistance to destruction by weathering or vandalism is often due to the sheer monumental volume of natural stone rather than to human ingenuity or concern.

In Britain the notable buildings of the Middle Ages were the parish churches, cathedrals, baronial halls and, later, the great country houses of the Elizabethan, Jacobean and Georgian eras.

In the first half of the eighteenth century, the major European buildings were still predominantly castles, palaces, churches and early town halls. However, in the latter half, and as the nineteenth century progressed, a proliferation of building types for every conceivable purpose appeared as the Industrial Revolution gained momentum: railway architecture, factories, mills, warehouses, hotels, hospitals, public libraries, schools, colleges, offices, dockland and mercantile buildings, theatres, prisons, music and concert halls, observatories and military establishments. This in addition to private dwellings, villas, apartment buildings—all producing unprecedented functional solutions and expressing architectural styles that were often adapted from classical or Gothic predecessors.

Despite the speed and extent of nineteenth-century urban development, many beautiful buildings took form. Often, they displayed the wealth or eased the consciences of those enriched by the mining, textile and other burgeoning industries and the banking and commerce they generated. We have private patronage to thank for most of the rich heritage of buildings, monuments and parks created during this exciting period when town planning and social justice were not government's primary concerns.

In 1895 the first of the historical and preservation organizations, the National Trust, was formed, its purpose being the permanent preservation of lands and buildings of historic interest. In 1926 the Council for the Preservation of Rural England (C.P.R.E.) emerged "to provide and encourage the improvement, protection and preservation of the English countryside and its towns and villages." Both bodies have had, and still do have, a great influence in conservation, but by their nature they reflected the fact that the heart of the educated classes was romantically in the countryside. The C.P.R.E. has done much to educate public opinion by way of conferences and exhibitions. In 1924 the Ancient Monuments Society had been founded: it now advises local authorities on the proposed demolition of listed buildings and on methods of preservation. In the same year, the Royal Fine Arts Commission was established. Today its principal concern is to influence good design in inner-city regeneration. Increasingly, more specialised societies have been formed, including the Georgian Group, the Irish Georgian Society, the Victorian Society, the Country Houses Association and the Vernacular Architecture Group.

The relative stability of the late nineteenth and early twentieth centuries led to a major increase in fine buildings. The growing

Opposite: The magnificent Chelsea Bridge, across the River Thames in London, at the turn of the century. Each of London's bridges has been modified during this century to meet the demands of ever-increasing traffic.

Opposite: *At the turn of the century the city of Liverpool, on the estuary of the River Mersey, had a busy commuter passenger ferry service between seven landing stages. The ferry terminal at the George's landing stage, shown in this 1937 photograph (now demolished), adjoined the customs hall for arriving ocean passengers at the Prince's landing stage. Although two ferries are still in operation today, the Mersey Tunnel is the major commuter crossing, and ocean crossings are almost entirely by air.*

The passenger ferry terminal, here thronged with commuters, was designed to cope with the enormous daily foot traffic of a busy commercial centre. The city has suffered a degree of economic decline since World War II, but it remains a lively educational and cultural centre.

involvement of government and new local authorities augmented public and private patronage in the development of town planning, public health and building legislation. Prior to this, many communities had grown haphazardly since the Civil War. In this context, the onset of World War II was a dramatic turning point in bringing the destruction of historic buildings, particularly in such urban centers as London, Liverpool, Coventry, Manchester and Bristol. The great blitzes of 1941 wreaked havoc, as some of the examples in this book illustrate.

Following the war, and a massive swing to more socially conscious policies, there would be new building and redevelopment on an unprecedented scale. Despite the reformist education, planning and building legislation of the postwar period, the nation was ill-equipped materially (for example, with shortages of good materials and skilled labour) and aesthetically (for example, inadequate control over design expertise) to avoid a rash of poor-quality building, particularly in the 1960s. The Treasury structure encouraged a rush for floor space, and consideration for quality of design and future maintenance were largely scorned.

There had been a much broader band of public involvement since the creation of the Civic Trust in 1957. Not only did it concern itself with conserving and improving the environment of town and countryside, it has promoted local societies whose vigilant conservation initiatives have overcome their earlier reputations as busybodies.

The collapse of the primary industries, the decline of the railways and public transport in the wake of the mass rush to car ownership, the decline of the churches—all have led to disuse of many fine buildings and a morass of destruction resulting from road widening, by-pass and motorway development and the subsequent decline in urban shopping and commerce when traffic congestion forced the development of out-of-town shopping and business parks. Overlaying this decline of the

urban scene was the hectic building boom of the 1980s, which produced massive multi-story office development in the cities.

These changes have done little in the cause of architecture, and now more than ever we need to preserve the best of the past and

adapt it alongside good contemporary design. To this end, strong legislation is now in place with respect to listed buildings. This is backed by English Heritage, formed in 1984, which is responsible for securing the preservation of England's architecture and heritage through the management of more than 350 monuments and buildings. Further, the English Historic Forum was set up in 1987 "to promote and reconcile prosperity and conservation in historic towns."

— KEITH HUNT

Dockside and Overhead Railway, Liverpool Above
The seat of the Industrial Revolution, Liverpool's wealth was built on importing raw materials and exporting the textiles and manufactured goods of industrial northern England to destinations all over the world. The second-largest British port (after London), her docks extended along five miles of the Mersey estuary and were linked to Manchester and other northern cities by canal. Nothing in this aerial view, dating from the early 1950s, remains today. The three chimneys in the background, known as "The Three Sisters," were demolished as recently as the early 1990s. This section of the docks is now used for parking; the overhead railway was torn down and the tunnel whose entrance was here is no longer used.

Euston Arch, London *Above*

The earliest railway station ever built in a capital city, Euston has unique significance in the development of the Railway Age. The enormous, striking arch, completed in 1838, was part of a complex designed by Philip Hardwick. Despite its status as a Grade II listed building, the Euston Arch (along with the entire station) was demolished in 1962 after a battle with conservationists, because the station was deemed outmoded and the costs of removing the Arch and restoring it at another location were too great. Public opposition to the demolition—dubbed the "Euston Murder"—was so great that subsequent plans to destroy and overhaul neighbouring St. Pancras, another monumental Victorian station, were abandoned.

Chelsea Bridge, London *Above*

Engineer Thomas Page designed this elegant structure,
which became the ninth bridge across the Thames in
the London area when it opened to traffic in 1858. The
suspension bridge originally had more ornamentation
than is shown in this 1929 photograph. The traffic
demands of twentieth-century London necessitated
the opening of several new bridges and, eventually, the
widening and/or rebuilding of all of those already in
existence. A modified Chelsea Bridge survives today,
retaining some of the features shown here.

The Coal Exchange, City of London *Above and right*
Opened by Prince Albert in 1849, the Coal Exchange
was designed by J.B. Bunning and celebrated as a
monument testifying to London's status as capital of
the financial world. The building's interior was
elaborately ornamented with both painted and
ironwork decoration. Despite its historic importance,
the Coal Exchange was earmarked for destruction by
traffic planners who implemented a road-widening
scheme that would save the Custom House, situated
across from the Coal Exchange on Lower Thames
Street. After a lengthy battle with conservationists, the
demolition went ahead in 1963, although the site
remained undeveloped and was used only for parking
for over a decade.

The Old King's Head, London *Opposite*
Situated at the intersection of Euston Road and
Hampstead Road, the fate of this classic 1880s-built
popular London pub was sealed by its location on two
major traffic routes. It was demolished in 1906 as part
of a road-widening scheme.

Temple Bar, The Strand, London *Above*
This 1870s photograph shows the eastern view down
the historic Strand—a street dating at least to Roman
times—through Temple Bar, built in 1672 and
attributed to Sir Christopher Wren. Much of the Strand
has been demolished and rebuilt during the twentieth
century; Temple Bar was removed as early as 1878 to
ease traffic flow.

Ramsgate Airport *Above*
One of three airports in the area, this innovative
structure designed by David Pleydell Bouverie was
built in 1935 and opened to air traffic in 1937. This
photograph, published in the *Architectural Review* in
January 1938, made the precocious Bouverie famous.
The terminal's construction was technologically
advanced for its time: the roof, a single concrete slab,
was supported by twenty-six steel columns; all internal
partitions were movable in order to accommodate the
airport's future expansion and changing needs. The
interior, which featured massive sliding doors of solid
teak, was designed and furnished by Alvar Aalto.
Ramsgate airport was closed to private flying at the
beginning of World War II, and, just a few years after
its opening, the terminal building was severely
damaged by enemy action.

Adelphi Terrace, London *Below*
The imposing Adelphi Terrace, consisting of elegant river-front houses built upon vaulted arches (just visible at lower right of this photograph), was built by the brothers Adam, who completed their grand scheme in 1774. The central pediment was a later addition to the classically designed terrace. During the 1930s, the "dull, square boxes" that typified Georgian architecture were regarded as a low conservation priority, and Adelphi Terrace fell victim to this attitude in 1937. Its destruction prompted the formation of the Georgian Group, a society dedicated to preserving eighteenth-century buildings.

Westminster Hospital, London *Above*
This photograph shows Westminster Hospital in its
third location and after some 1870s modifications to
the building's original 1834 design by William Inwood.
Despite modernisation, the hospital became
unworkable as demand increased and medical science
developed. This building was finally demolished in
1951, when the hospital was once again relocated.

Columbia Market, Bethnal Green, London *Below*
Baroness Burdett-Coutts sponsored the construction of
this lavish folly, the covered Columbia Market, which
was designed in 1864 by Henry Darbishire. The market
was part of a philanthropic regeneration scheme for
this working-class area of London's East End. A
financial flop, the market closed in 1885. London
County Council bought the complex and eventually, in
the 1960s, demolished it to make way for a housing
development.

New Street, Birmingham *Above*

Visitors in Birmingham's city centre today would
recognise nothing in this 1895 photograph of New
Street, which was extensively bomb-damaged during
World War II and redeveloped with modern, clinical
offices and commercial buildings during the 1960s.
This lively scene shows primarily nineteenth-century
buildings including the Free Grammar School, the
Gothic-revival building on the left side of the street,
which was designed by Charles Barry and Augustus
Welby Pugin—the architects of Westminster Palace.

Five Ways, Birmingham *Above*
This 1920 view of Birmingham's Five Ways features
Georgian houses and, on the right, a white Portland
stone bank building designed by P.B. Chatwin in 1908.
During the nineteenth century, this area was part of
Birmingham's boundary; Five Ways was a toll gate. A
1960s shopping complex and major overhead road
junction now stand on this site.

St. Enoch's, Glasgow
Miss Cranston's Tea Rooms, Glasgow *Previous pages*
Imposing Victorian civic, university and residential
tenement buildings dominate the skyline of this
bustling city, but it is perhaps best known
architecturally for the work of Charles Rennie
Mackintosh (1868–1928) and his colleagues, who were
responsible for the Arts-and-Crafts era "Glasgow
Style." Mackintosh's interior design for Miss
Cranston's Tea Rooms (demolished) exemplify his
style, which was an important precursor of Art
Nouveau. St. Enoch's Square in the city centre was
dominated by the railway station, one of four mainline
stations in Glasgow until the major network cuts
implemented in the late 1960s, and the station hotel.
After the station's close, the hotel's business declined,
and both buildings were demolished in the late 1970s.
A large modern shopping centre, opened in May 1989,
now stands on the site.

Alloa House *Above*
The twentieth century has seen the decline of Britain's
aristocracy and a drastic change in lifestyle for most of
those who retained their ancestral homes, which
proved too expensive and impractical for all but a few
to maintain. In a fate typical of such families, the
owners of Alloa House left their home in 1955 and
attempted to negotiate with the local council a suitable
new use for the building. Despite the efforts of the
National Trust and other conservation bodies, many
stately homes have not been preserved, because of the
prohibitive costs of restoration. Alloa House was
demolished in 1965.

Odeon Cinema, Surbiton Above

This vintage Art Deco structure, designed by Joseph Hill and built in 1934 in the London suburb of Surbiton, was typical of British cinemas during their heyday earlier this century, when they were often a focal point of the urban street. The rise of television led to the postwar decline of cinema attendance and the routine destruction or alteration of cinemas, often for use as bingo halls. Modern multiscreen centres are now becoming commonplace around the country.

James Street Station, Liverpool *Opposite*
This photograph shows the tower and partial bridge
balustrade of James Street Station, all that remained of
the building after its devastation by a World War II
bomb. British Rail subsequently pulled down these
remains and redeveloped the station site.

Head Post Office, Liverpool *Above*
This impressive building, located at the corner of
Victoria Street and Sir Thomas Street, suffered two
bouts of bomb damage, in March and May 1941. The
upper part of the building was badly damaged,
although the shell of the lower storeys has remained
virtually intact, essentially unchanged since this 1940s
photograph was taken. Unused for over fifty years, the
site is now designated for redevelopment as a city-
centre shopping facility.

The Crystal Palace *Above and left*

Originally built in 1850 in London's Hyde Park to house the Great Exhibition, the technically advanced iron-and-glass Crystal Palace was designed by a team of architects and engineers headed by Sir Joseph Paxton, and its huge, partly prefabricated frame was erected with the help of horse-operated cranes. Often referred to as the first major work of modern architecture, the "blazing arch of lucid glass" was visited by over six million people during 1851. After the exhibition's close, Crystal Palace was removed to a permanent site in Sydenham, south London, where it was reconstructed, extended and adapted as a recreational and educational hall in a public park. One of Britain's best-known architectural treasures, the building was destroyed by fire in 1936.

The Chain Pier, Brighton *Above*
Brighton's graceful Chain Pier was built in 1823 and immediately became a landmark of this popular seaside tourist town. This structure, too, fell victim to natural disaster: it was extensively damaged by fire in 1833 but was restored, only to be destroyed in 1896 by a severe storm.

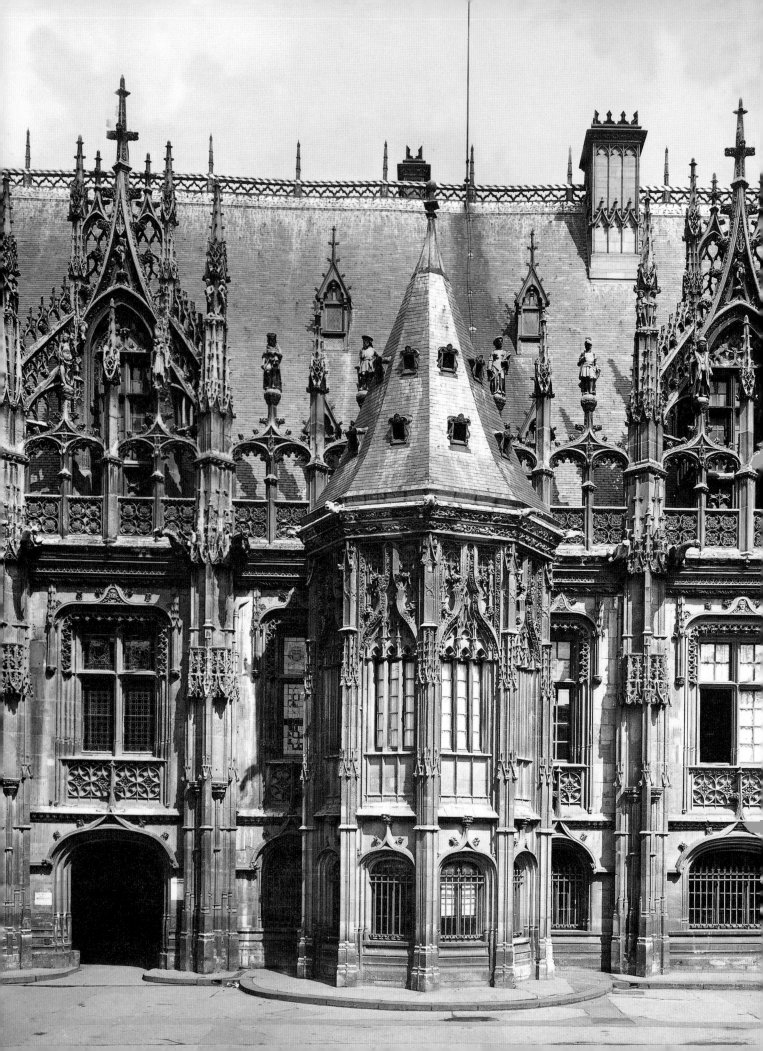

France

The second largest and one of the oldest countries in Europe, France has a rich cultural heritage that confirms her unique reputation as the "museum of Europe." Maintaining this rich and diverse wealth of art and architecture through a century of rapid social, industrial and economic upheaval has not been a simple task. In addition to the demands of "progress" and modernisation, much of the twentieth century has been devoted to recuperating from the physical and economic disarray resulting from the widespread destruction of both World Wars.

When World War I began in August 1914, the French believed that the war with the Germans would be a brief conflict, readily and swiftly resolved. What they did not expect was a four-year war of attrition that would change forever the nature of warfare and cause such architectural devastation as well as countless deaths. World War I officially ended on June 28, 1919, with the signing of the Treaty of Versailles—a document that also sowed the seeds of World War II.

France watched as Hitler rose to power in Germany in 1933. That same year Germany withdrew from the League of Nations, an organization accepted by the signatories to the Treaty of Versailles. Two years later Hitler introduced compulsory military service, and in 1936 the Rhineland was reoccupied and militarisation had begun again in earnest— and in defiance of the Treaty of Versailles.

The realisation that another war was unavoidable came in August 1939, when the Nazi-Soviet Pact was signed, and confirmed that September when Germany invaded Poland. France and Great Britain declared war on Germany on September 3, when Hitler ignored their demand for German withdrawal from Poland. The next eight months saw few engagements, and the "phony war," as it was called, lulled the French into a false sense of security. On May 10, 1940, the Germans attacked France through the Ardennes Forest. By May 20, they had reached the coast and successfully encircled French and British troops, who were forced to evacuate by sea from Dunkirk. By June 15, Paris had fallen.

After the fall of France, the government fled to Bordeaux, where the Chamber of Deputies voted power to Henri Philippe Pétain, the eighty-four-year-old marshal of France. Great Britain released France from her agreement to go on fighting, and on June 22, 1940, France surrendered to the Germans, who occupied the northern and western sections of the country. The south remained unoccupied, and the Vichy government was established with Pétain as chief of state.

Due to the very swift conquest by the Germans, France suffered relatively little physical damage until June 1944, when the Allied invasion of Europe was launched from Normandy, the northwestern region that extends along the English Channel (*La Manche*) between Picardy and Brittany. This historic region of farmlands and fishermen comprised cities and towns dating back to the Norman conquest of England in 1066, when William, Duke of Normandy, crossed the Channel to subdue the Saxons. Norman church architecture derived its inspiration from the Romanesque churches of the Christian era that began about AD 300, when the new religion was spreading throughout western Europe. Bold and massive, the

Opposite: The Law Courts (Palais de Justice) *at Rouen, begun in 1499, probably by Roger Ango and Rolland Le Roux. The building contained the renowned timber-vaulted Attorneys' Hall* (Salle des Pas Perdus)*. It was destroyed during World War II.*

Above: *Beautifully preserved Norman buildings at Lisieux were among the casualties of the Allied invasion of 1944.*

Norman style is characterized by short, heavy columns supporting semicircular arches and square towers. Decorative geometric patterns, including zigzags, were originally hewn with axes; more sophisticated carvings were perfected over time.

Other architectural treasures of Normandy included medieval civic centres, fortifications and guild halls and such Renaissance structures as the Town Hall at Cassel, used as the headquarters of General Foch during World War I, which was completely destroyed. Additional casualties of the fighting in Normandy were the Court Room at Rouen—the capital of the old province—which had once been the Hall of Parliament and the Law Courts, begun in 1499 by the architects Roger Ango and Rolland Le Roux. Rouen's Cathedral of Notre-Dame was heavily damaged. Comparable losses were suffered in other cities, including Caen and Bayeux.

The ancient city of Marseilles came under attack as a major port, and the waterfront, including the City Hall (1663–83), was levelled by air raids. Countless towns and villages were damaged or destroyed as the Germans retreated. Paris was retaken by the Allies in August 1944, and the Germans finally surrendered on May 7, 1945, after

their country had been bombed repeatedly and invaded along two fronts, which eventually converged at Berlin.

World War I had been called the "war to end all wars," but the devastation that France experienced during World War II was unprecedented. More than half the railways had been destroyed, making it almost impossible to travel throughout the country. Equally catastrophic was the toll of structures that had exemplified the architectural glory of France, many razed to the ground, others surviving as burnt-out shells. Reconstruction was undertaken after the war, but many cultural monuments could not be salvaged, much less replaced.

Having suffered such extensive destruction in two wars (and further problems during the Algerian crisis), one of the first priorities of General Charles de Gaulle, the charismatic leader voted president in the landslide 1958 election that also confirmed the constitution for the Fifth Republic, was to modernise the country and stabilise her weakened economy. De Gaulle and his successor, Georges Pompidou (from 1969), concentrated on the much-needed rebuilding of infrastructure and demands of industry, sometimes, of necessity, at the expense of conservation and restoration.

President Pompidou was himself responsible for commissioning one of the most controversial modern structures in the land: the *Centre National d'Art et de Culture Georges Pompidou* (Ove Arup and Partners, architects, completed 1978) in the Beaubourg district of central Paris. The monumental, brightly coloured "inside-out" structure—whose frame of tubular steel and mechanical systems, including escalators and utility conduits, are all visible on the building's exterior—stood in stark contrast to its surroundings and shocked conservationists. Central Paris had been transformed during the mid-nineteenth century by urban planner Georges Eugène Haussmann, who devised and implemented an ambitious modernisation plan consisting of wide boulevards, parks and new civic buildings that replaced the narrow streets and buildings of earlier eras. The distinctive and cohesive character of Haussmann's reconstructed Paris made the city a model for urban planners worldwide.

The Pompidou Centre is one of a number of postwar urban renovation projects in Paris, including the clearance of the nearby *Les Halles*, a food market originally dating from the twelfth century that had been rebuilt during the Haussmann era. The market was replaced by a modern shopping complex known as the *Forum des Halles*. The skyscrapers of *La Défense* and the *Tour Montparnasse* in the old Bohemian quarter south of the city's centre are further examples.

Perhaps the most famous recent change to a Parisian landmark is the addition of the celebrated glass pyramid designed by I.M. Pei to the stately, world-renowned museum, the Louvre. Originally a palace dating from the twelfth century, the Louvre consists of a complex of buildings that are mainly French Renaissance in style, rebuilt and extended over a period of several centuries. Pei's addition (along with a new underground section housing restaurants, shops, museum administration and educational facilities) was commissioned in 1984 by the government as part of an expansion and modernisation plan. The alterations, while preserving the former sections, raised complex questions for conservationists; paradoxically, Pei himself is renowned for his sensitivity to environmental appropriateness in his approach to design.

Outside of the capital, many other towns and cities around the country have changed significantly during the postwar period. Numerous picturesque frontages and street corners have disappeared to make way for bigger and better roads. Functional modern structures have replaced old, traditional houses, offices and shopping facilities. Tourism, too, has provided the impetus for new commercial construction, although much has been safeguarded because a large

part of the appeal for tourists is France's rich heritage of buildings dating from many centuries past.

Architectural preservation poses many pragmatic difficulties and must be balanced against considerations of economy, modernisation and efficiency of space. Conservationists are sometimes criticised for failing to address these questions; they are criticised, too, on an aesthetic level—for failing to embrace new developments in design or to accept the concept of change itself. A number of France's most influential architectural landmarks are modern designs: the Art Nouveau designs of Hector Guimard, built mainly between 1890 and 1910, are examples. Change cannot and should not be avoided, but must be modified by a keen sense of what is lost in the process.

Much remains to be done to strengthen France's legislation and commitment to historic preservation, a goal that can be accomplished while yet accepting the value of the contributions made by architects of the modern period and, indeed, the contemporary and future artists whose visions are yet to be realised. This imperative is vital to France, not because her conservation record is lacking, so much as because of her uniquely valuable manmade riches.

—Jean Loussier

Above: *Rouen, the capital of Normandy since 912, lost many medieval buildings between the damaged Cathedral of Notre-Dame and the Seine and in the area north and east of the Law Courts.*

Church of Saint-Gilles, Caen *Opposite*
Damaged during World War I, this ancient church,
dating from the seventh century and rebuilt later,
combined Gothic and Romanesque elements. It was
destroyed during World War II.

Escoville Mansion, Caen *Above*
This noble example of French Renaissance
architecture, built in the mid-sixteenth century by the
architect Blaise Le Prestre, was nearly razed by
bombing in 1944. Nicolas le Valois, seigneur
d'Escoville, and a descendant of Charles le Valois
(1270–1325), commissioned the house.

Paris, Les Halles Centrales *Opposite*

Two views of the ten-acre city market, built on a site in use as a food market since the twelfth century. The prominent architect Victor Baltard (1805–74) constructed the original ten pavilions of cast iron and glass between 1854–70. The photograph below dates from the late 1800s, the one above from about 1920; further pavilions were added in 1936. The entire area was cleared in 1973. It was redeveloped as a fashionable shopping centre known as *Forum des Halles,* and the food market was relocated in the suburb of Rungis.

Paris, Bohemian Montmartre *Right*

The Moulin de la Galette in its heyday: a restaurant and a mecca for *habitués* of this literary and artistic district. The last remaining seventeenth-century windmill in the area, the building has been preserved, but its ambience and surroundings have altered and its glamour faded.

The Trocadéro Palace *Below*

Built for the Paris Exhibition of 1878, the Trocadéro Palace was designed by G.-J.-A. Davioud (1823–81) and torn down in the 1920s.

9. BOBIGNY. — Place de l'Eglise.   J. L. C.

The Way We Were

Above and opposite

Dating from the first decade of the twentieth century, these evocative photographs reflect a time before the pace of life became hurried. The scenes shown here are nostalgic; few of the buildings remain, and the ambience has vanished in each case.

   None of the structures in the period view above of the *Place de l'Église* (Church Square) in Bobigny, located just outside Paris, have survived to the end of the century. In the early 1970s a utilitarian high-rise building was erected behind the church. Since then, the church has been replaced with a modern, windowless, concrete church building, and the shops in the foreground razed for a wider road and a park. The area is now known as the Quartier Karl-Marx.

Before the introduction of cars, trams were a common means of transport in towns and cities; tram tracks are visible in this view of the *Grand Rue* (Main Road) in Chaville, shown opposite, above. With the gradual increase in car ownership, streets have been widened and improved, and few tracks remain. The café was the first of the buildings in this scene to be redeveloped, and the rest of the block soon followed. Today, two modern apartment buildings occupy their places.

   Bustling street scenes like this one (opposite, below) on the Rue du Bac in Suresnes, a western suburb of Paris, are quintessentially French, and pedestrian cafés could once be found in most villages and small towns. Though most of the buildings on the left of this busy street are still standing, the right side fell victim to a traffic-efficiency scheme that includes a roundabout and parking area.

SURESNES -- Rue du Bac et Place Henri IV   E.L.D.

Modernist Commercial Architecture *Above*
Architect Auguste Perret, a pioneer in the use of reinforced-concrete construction, designed this Parisian clothing factory, now demolished, in 1919. Perret also built the Théâtre des Champs-Elysées in Paris between 1911 and 1913.

Vintage Hector Guimard *Opposite and left*
Early twentieth-century works by this gifted Art Nouveau architect included the Hotel de Léon Nazal (opposite, above), constructed in Paris in 1902. At left is the Place de la Bastille entrance to the original Paris underground railway (1900). Seventeen of the *Métro* entrances designed by Guimard (1867–1942) remain.

The Netherlands

The twentieth century has seen drastic and rapid changes both in the Dutch landscape—for example, the Wieringermeerpolder, the Noordoostpolder and Flevoland have been "won from the sea"—and in building construction and infrastructure. Since the turn of the century, when H.P. Berlage's Commodity Exchange was built, many exceptional buildings have been constructed. Equally striking, however, is the long list of characteristic buildings that have disappeared from the Dutch landscape.

When one looks for possible reasons for this, the proverbial Dutch mania for having everything neat and tidy springs immediately to mind. Other factors, also at work in other European countries, including technical advances, mobility, commerce, secularisation, the ravages of time or—to a lesser degree in the Netherlands—war and natural disasters, can also be indicated. Technical developments, for example, wrought havoc with the country's mills. Steam engines, diesel motors and later, electricity, replaced wind and water power. In the middle of the nineteenth century, the Netherlands still had about 10,000 mills: today, only about 1,000 survive.

The explosive increase in mobility in the twentieth century is reflected in the countless canals that have been filled in, breakthroughs in urban construction, countless kilometres of metalled roads and ambitious circulation schemes. A great deal disappeared quite unnecessarily because such schemes were delayed or scrapped altogether, or were carried out in a much modified form.

Economic motives almost always play a prominent role. The most powerful argument for demolition often appears to be the value of the land, or the notion that building anew is a cheaper solution than restoration. In the first half of this century, a growing population and increasing purchasing power formed the basis of a flourishing shop architecture. Many of these often beautiful shopfronts and interiors have disappeared as a result of an increase in scale, changes in taste and competitive rivalry.

After the episcopal hierarchy was restored in the Netherlands in 1853, hundreds of churches, very many in Neo-Gothic style, soon appeared throughout the country as beacons of the reborn Roman Catholic faith. Secularisation, which intensified in the years after World War II, signalled the end for many of these houses of worship. Since the 1960s, the interiors of those churches that had survived the mathematics of standing empty and increasing land values have regularly been the victims of a twentieth-century iconoclasm. The battle to bring religious experience "closer to the people," in particular, resulted in the disfiguration of a great number of richly furnished and sacrally significant church interiors.

The degree to which the ravages of time affect monuments and historic buildings has, of course, a great deal to do with maintenance, the materials used in construction and their intended purpose. Many more recent buildings, for example, now face problems because when they were built—between 1910 and 1930—experimental techniques and newly emergent materials like steel and concrete were used. Between the two World Wars, semi-permanent complexes designed to alleviate the severe housing shortage sprang up all over the Netherlands. Mode of construction, materials used and dimensions were all determined on the basis that they would have a relatively short lifespan.

Opposite: Imposing seventeenth-century windmills along the Zaanstreek, once part of a thriving industrial centre on De Hemmes Peninsula.

53

Above: Amsterdam, the former Beursplein, circa 1890: The house just visible on the right was demolished in 1903 to make way for an art dealer's premises. The characteristic buildings on the other side of the alley disappeared for a shop and office complex that opened in 1913. The block of houses on the higher-lying Beurspleintje was demolished in 1914 to make way for the "Industria" building.

During World War II (1939–45), the historic inner cities of Rotterdam, Middelburg, Nijmegen, Arnhem and Groningen were destroyed. During the war years approximately 300 historic buildings were literally reduced to rubble.

The worst natural disaster to ravage the Netherlands in this century was the storm tide on the night of January 31–February 1, 1953. Repair and rebuilding of the destroyed and damaged buildings was to a large extent assimilated into the postwar reconstruction programmes. These plans had already been partly prepared during the war years to facilitate rebuilding of destroyed town and village centres and to repair more than a thousand damaged monuments and historic buildings. The opportunity to rebuild these new centres according to the most modern plans and perceptions was seized upon gratefully. However, the zeal for modernisation was tempered by conservative sanctions.

Preservation of Monuments and Historic Buildings in the Netherlands

It was only late in the nineteenth century that growing historical interest led to governmental involvement in the preservation of monuments and historic buildings. Documenting and describing worthy buildings had long been the task of interested and often enthusiastic amateurs. There were also frequent protests against the "mad urge to demolish." In 1873 the militant lawyer Victor de Steurs published *"Holland op zijn smalst"* ("Holland at the peak of small-mindedness"), the latest in a long line of biting protests against everything and everyone that threatened the national heritage. But this time the protest proved effective—a year later the *College van de Rijksadviseurs voor de Monumenten van Geschiedenis en Kunst* (Government Advisory Commission for Historical and Artistic Monuments) was set up, and 1875 saw the

birth of the Arts and Sciences Department at the Ministry of Home Affairs. In 1903 a government commission was established to draw up an inventory of monuments and historic buildings. Five years later, this commission produced a first *Voorlopige Lijst der Nederlandsche Monumenten van Geschiedenis en Kunst* (Provisional List of Dutch Historical and Artistic Monuments). When the *"Rijksbureau voor de Monumentenzorg"* (Government Office for the Preservation of Monuments and Historic Buildings) was eventually created, in 1918, it had a department that was specially concerned with restoration.

All these developments were fuelled by vehement discussions on exactly how monuments and historic buildings should be treated. In 1917 fundamental principles were laid down which, in essence, advocated "conservative restoration," a way of thinking that had already been propagated at the

end of the eighteenth century. This fundamental principle was exhaustively argued as recently as the 1980s in the *Restauratienota 1982 (Restoration Memorandum 1982)*. The basic point that the value of a building as an original, irreplaceable historical source is the first matter of importance is summarized. That is to say that preservation precedes modernisation, and that additions or alterations must be designed in a recognisable form. Moreover, such interventions must be reversible. Existing restoration work should be respected because it is part of the history of the building. In the case of a change of function, the significance of the building is considered the deciding factor.

Shortly after the German invasion in May 1940, the Dutch Commander-in-Chief, General Winkelman, as the representative of the government, issued a number of decrees regarding reconstruction. For the

Above: Amsterdam—Dam, Zocher's Exchange (photograph circa 1890s): No photograph survives of Amsterdam's first commodity exchange, designed by Hendrick de Keyser, which was demolished in 1835. Its successor was the splendid Neo-Classical building at right, designed by architect J.D. Zocher (1845). It was replaced in 1903 by H.P. Berlage's famous Commodity Exchange.

first time in the Netherlands, there was a question of legal protection for monuments and historic buildings. A few other provisional regulations followed this *"Besluit Wederopbouw I"* (Reconstruction Decree I). Eventually, in 1961, the first *"Monumentenwet"* (Historic Buildings and Ancient Monuments Act) came into force. This has since been superseded by the Act of 1988, in which a sharper difference is drawn between government policy and that of the provinces and municipalities. Potential national monuments must still be at least fifty years old, but lesser authorities can use their own judgement in determining whether this rule should apply when designating a monument or historic building.

The much-criticised fifty-year limit meant that until the beginning of the 1970s, the so-called younger architecture was largely ignored. It was only after the demolition of the Tilburg textile factory "Pieter van Dooren" in 1975 that any real attention was paid to historic monuments of business and technology. This came too late to save, for example, the South Limburg coal mining region. In 1978 the Government Department for the Preservation of Monuments and Historic Buildings began a gigantic inventory of more recent architecture (the Monument Inventory Project) which is now in its final selection and registration phase.

A Modern Dilemma:
Protected, Preserved, Damaged
In December 1979, the former convalescent home "De Blauwvoet" was demolished. A little later, on January 1, 1980, this elegant, whitewashed little building, in austere business style, would have become a protected building. The same thing happened in 1995 to another building designed by the same architect—J.B. van Loghem. His villa in Waalre was also demolished, because the owner was afraid he could forget about his new plans for it once it had been declared an official listed building. In other words a mere indication that a building may be

designated a monument can itself be the catalyst that expedites demolition.

During the 1980s, the Neo-Gothic Sacred Heart Church in Vondelstraat, Amsterdam, one of the best works of architect P. J. H. Cuypers, was saved at the last moment. This gave cause for satisfaction, but the campaign group was also disappointed about the valuable things that were lost, particularly in the interior. The complaint *"from sacred heart to sacred feasibility"* strikingly illustrates a real dilemma in the preservation of monuments and historic buildings in the Netherlands: the building itself is preserved, but is its value as an *historic* building also preserved?

Changing its purpose can also "demolish" an historic building without actually knocking it down. Former churches are particularly popular as apartment complexes, because a great number of units can be fitted into the large spaces. Slowly, a standard "solution" has evolved whereby only the silhouette and walls remain whole: historic and architectural values have disappeared completely from the picture.

The Historic Buildings and Ancient Monuments Act of 1961 recognised the possibility of designating protected towns and villages. The neighbouring environment is also important for individual buildings. In particular, filling in canals, breakthroughs in urban development, deviant heights of buildings or plot widths and new buildings which do not conform can create disastrous effects to their environments.

There is often an enormous gulf between theoretical principles and restoration practice. The notion of "conservative restoration" is regularly transgressed, as can be seen from the restoration of, for example, Het Loo Palace in Apeldoorn, Noordeinde Palace in The Hague or the Sint-Servaas Church in Maastricht. Another fundamental principle of restoration, the "recognisably contemporary" design of new elements, is sometimes taken so far that the essential character of the historic building itself is completely overshadowed.

A Balance

The importance and care of the built-up environment in the Netherlands has long been supported by private initiative. At the moment, some 700 institutions and organisations of one form or another are active in this field. Open Monument Days—based on the French model—have been organised in the Netherlands since September 1987. Thanks partly to their accessible nature, these events attract many visitors—in 1996, an estimated 700,000. The various preservation campaigns during recent years also indicate wider public support. Of course, this does not always have to do with "beauty, scientific significance or cultural historical value," as the Historic Buildings and Ancient Monuments Act of 1988 so nicely puts it, but simply with what is close at hand and what is considered important by local residents.

The government still has an important task. The protection of "monument value" is threatened by the pandemonium of divergent aspects on which plans are judged, the ever-limited financial resources and the expected flood of more recent,

more ordinary, industrial monuments. To give an indication of the "catching up operation": in 1994 more than 43,000 buildings were officially protected, while the Monument Inventory Project noted some 165,000 valuable and several hundred exceptional complexes and regions. The Government Department for the Preservation of Monuments and Historic Buildings plays a prominent role in matters of protection, laying down laws and regulations, giving advice, carrying out research and disseminating information. But government can also be expected to guide and to play an exemplary role in awarding commissions and in building control. Prospects in this field, unfortunately, are sombre; dark clouds, for example, are gathering above reconstruction architecture. In 1950–53 the building for the Ministry of Education, Arts and Sciences was built in Den Haag (The Hague). This building, designed by government architect G. Friedhoff, full of historical and symbolic associations in the design language of post-war traditionalism, was demolished in 1996.

—Jos Smit

Above: Leeuwarden, 't Vliet (circa late 1940s). The Vliet became an important trade route during the Middle Ages and flourished from the seventeenth century, when many handsome buildings rose along the waterway. The canal was filled in, with destruction of the entire street, as the result of a 1969–70 improvement scheme that proved, with hindsight, to have been unnecessary.

Amsterdam, Mauritsstraat 1–9,
"Piece of Pie" Building Opposite

Aptly nicknamed, this wedge-shaped house on
Weesperzijde (photographed in 1932) was so
constructed because of its narrow location between
the Amstel and the tracks of a freight railway to the
Weesperpoort Station. The design for this block of
houses, by J.J. van de Bilt, was approved in April 1881.
In 1961 the whole uneven-numbered side of
Mauritsstraat was demolished for an ambitious road-
improvement scheme that included the new Toronto
Bridge. The low building on the left was the freight
warehouse for the former Weesperpoort Station.

Amsterdam, Weesperpoort Station Above

In 1843 King Willem III opened the Rhijnspoor
Station—several detached, Classical buildings
designed by railway engineer J.A. v.d. Kun. This station
was soon rebuilt and extended. The high roof above
the platforms—formed by crescent-shaped iron
ribs—was completed in 1863. Amsterdam
Weesperpoort, as the Rhijnspoor Station was later
known, remained the city's largest until the landmark
Central Station was built. As Amsterdam grew still
larger and rail traffic burgeoned, the street-level
station became an obstacle. Amsterdam Weesperpoort
(photographed in 1937) closed on October 14, 1939, a
day after the Amstel and Muiderpoort Stations came
into use, and was then demolished.

Utrecht, Central Station *Above*
Central Station in Utrecht, completed in 1940, shortly
before this photograph was taken, was a gem of
aesthetic/practical architecture. Using such materials
as concrete, steel, chrome and extensive glass,
engineer Sybold van Ravesteyn designed a pure,
spacious building combining decorative forms and
an expressive silhouette. The bright interior afforded
luxurious facilities for dining and ample waiting
areas. Statues on the ridge-piece, designed by Mari
Andriessen, represented Security, Phoenix and Speed.
In 1975 Central Station had to make way for the Hoog-
Catharijne, a station complex including shops, offices
and catering that was apparently intended for "the
new caveman."

Utrecht, Leidseweg, Head Office "De Utrecht" and Archive Building *Above*

Here, two successful, but dissimilar, examples of modern architecture were constructed one after the other and photographed circa 1909. The new head office of the life insurance company "De Utrecht," designed by architect J. Verheul Dzn, came into service in 1902. It was one of the Netherlands' most beautiful examples of the New Art—a mixture of mobile Art Nouveau and abstract motifs. Verheul also created a detailed interior design, specifying furniture and decorative elements. In 1908 the adjacent brick Archive Building was constructed after an elegant, fireproof design by A.J. Kropholler and J.F. Staal. Both buildings were demolished in 1974 to make way for Hoog-Catharijne.

Bladel H.U.de
Koninginne 1904.

Eindhoven, "Hof van Holland" *Above*

In 1610 "De Grote Ster," later called the "Hof van Holland," was built in Rechtestraat. As photographed circa 1918, its prominent features included the *piano nobile*—the most important floor raised a little above street level—and the double stepped gables. In 1960 this beautiful building had to make way for construction of a modern fashion house.

Eindhoven, Town Hall *Opposite*

The Town Hall on Rechtestraat (photographed in 1904) was completed in 1869 after the design of municipal architect J.A. van Dijck. The Neo-Gothic style of this secular building is unusual because this language of form had been confined to new churches. Although this Town Hall was unique in the Netherlands, it was demolished in 1967 for the sake of a traffic scheme that was, in fact, never carried out.

Zaandam and the De Hemmes Peninsula

Opposite and below

From the beginning of the seventeenth century, the Zaanstreek grew into one of the world's largest industrial landscapes, lined with imposing warehouses and trade centres. A multicoloured diversity of windmills served to grind corn, press oil, saw wood and hull barley. In the course of the nineteenth century, many mills were demolished or were converted to steam power. Most of the seventeenth-century mills, warehouses and offices on De Hemmes, a peninsula in the Zaan, survived into the twentieth century, but within fifty years they had disappeared: moved elsewhere, burned down or demolished. These photographs date from the first decade of the century.

Scheveningen, Aerial View *Above*

This aerial photograph shows the Netherlands' first seaside resort, originally an unpretentious fishing village on the North Sea near The Hague, at the height of its popularity. A contemporary account describes it as having "many graceful buildings in a style of spa-resort beachside architecture typical of its era, the late nineteenth and early twentieth century." They included the Hotel Rauch, Grand Hotel Garni, Hotel des Galeries, Kurhaus, Palace Hotel, Oranjehotel, the theatre-café Seinpost, the Circus Cascade and various shopping arcades built in the neighbourhood of the Strandweg (Boulevard). Enforced closure during World War II and the increasing popularity of day trips made drastic measures necessary—according to the property developers. Thanks to local campaigns, the Kurhaus was eventually saved.

Boulevard and Promenade Pier Wilhelmina
Opposite, above

A promenade pier was opened on May 8, 1901, almost forty years after the first plans had been drawn up. Designed by W.B. van Liefland and E. Wyhofski, the pier began opposite the Kurhaus and was some 415 metres long and 8 metres wide. Parties, concerts and variety shows were held in its beautiful pavilion. Fire broke out in March 1943, and a year later Liefland's festive Art-Nouveau creation was demolished.

Hotel Garni, 1867 *Opposite, below*

Scheveningen's development into an international resort began in 1818 with the opening of a simple wooden bathhouse. Forty years later, a few people from The Hague decided to build a cheap hotel. Architect E. Saraber designed the Hotel Garni, which had 200 rooms, offered only bed and breakfast, and faced the beach. The Grand Hotel Garni, as it was known after major rebuilding in 1873–75, was demolished in 1974. The bathing machines in the foreground were drawn into the sea so that guests could enjoy the therapeutic powers of the water in privacy.

Scheveningen, Palace Hotel *Opposite*
In the second half of the nineteenth century, seaside holidays became very popular with the general public. The first deck chairs and beach tents appeared, the beach wall was erected and shopping arcades appeared along the Boulevard. Slowly, an almost unbroken row of hotels was created along the coast. A number of villas were demolished to accommodate the Palace Hotel, designed by W.B. van Liefland and built in 1903–04.

Boulevard, Palace Hotel and Oranjehotel *Above*
The Palace Hotel rose quickly, thanks to its modern concrete armature. Van Liefland designed a rich interior in various styles for the exuberant Art-Nouveau building of white stone. The hotel was demolished in 1979. The Hôtel d'Orange, in the background, designed by Cornelis Outshoorn, was built in 1860. During the war, it was so badly damaged by a bomb that it had to be demolished in 1952. The shopping arcade along the front, the *Oranjegalerij* by van Liefland (1903), disappeared during World War II to accommodate the Atlantic Wall.

Rotterdam, St. Laurenskerk *Opposite and above*
Rotterdam's historic inner city was largely destroyed
by the Luftwaffe bombing raids of May 14, 1940.
A modern city centre was designed with the "empty
space" as the point of departure. Only around the
Grotekerk—St. Laurens' Church, the most significant
landmark of Rotterdam's old quarter— did historic
considerations play a role in the reconstruction plans.
The church was begun early in the fifteenth century
and the spire completed in the seventeenth century.
All that remained after 1940 were parts of the walls
and the badly damaged spire. Some suggested that
the church should be preserved as a ruin, others that
the spire be retained and a separate, modern church
be built alongside it. Eventually, St. Laurenskerk was
reconstructed on the basis of old illustrations.

Amsterdam, Paleis voor Volksvlijt *Above*

The Paleis voor Volksvlijt, a permanent exhibition centre for Dutch industry, agriculture, trade and education, was opened on August 16, 1864. The splendid Paleis was comparable to London's Crystal Palace, although more traditional in style and materials. The architect, Cornelis Outshoorn, designed a "monumental structure" in Renaissance forms: 126 metres long, 80 metres wide and 62 metres tall. Over the years, the Paleis offered theatre, ballet and cabaret performances. Concerts and demonstrations were held, and it housed cafés and a roller-skating rink. A shopping arcade and housing were built along the edges of the garden. During the night of April 17–18, 1929, Amsterdam's "most photographed building" was badly damaged by fire. At the beginning of the 1960s, its remains were demolished to make way for the new premises of the Nederlandse Bank.

Amsterdam, De Korendrager Warehouse *Above*
The eighteenth-century façade of De Korendrager, on the Oude Schans, united three seventeenth-century warehouses, each about 30 metres deep and with four storage lofts above the lower frontage. The brick façade had rows of large shuttered windows flanked by smaller windows to provide light and air. Above the central axis was a hoisting hook for raising goods and supplies to the upper floors. This method is so practical that Amsterdam houses are still often furnished with such hooks. De Korendrager was destroyed by fire in 1949.

Rotterdam, De Koninginnekerk (Queen's Church) *Opposite and above*
The Koninginnekerk on Boezemsingel came into use in 1907. The two architects,
B. Hooykaas and M. Brinkman, produced a fairly severe design embellished by Neo-
Roman, Byzantine and other motifs. The church boasted excellent acoustics, and after
the nearby de Doelen Concert Hall was bombed in 1941, it was also used as a concert
hall (to 1969). The gradual secularisation of the community and decline in church
attendance led to the sale of the land for construction of a home for the elderly.
Despite attempts to save it, the church was demolished in January 1972.

Belgium

Belgium has earned the nickname "the cockpit of Europe" because of her long history of serving as a battle zone for European countries. A territory where the European balance of power was resolved, Belgium has been the site of more major European battles than any other comparable area. The consequences that Belgium has faced because of her unsolicited involvement in wars are immeasurable, but it was the occupation of Belgium by the Germans in both World Wars I and II that created the most architectural, economic and social devastation.

In 1815 the Congress of Vienna created the Kingdom of the Netherlands when it united Belgium and Holland, an alliance that lasted for fifteen years. In 1831 Belgium became an independent kingdom with a constitutional monarchy. In an attempt to avoid involvement in European conflicts, Belgium declared herself a neutral country, a stance that was reiterated in the Treaty of London in 1839, which stated that Belgium was "an independent and perpetually neutral state." However, Belgium's close proximity to France provided the Germans with an opportunity for attack that overshadowed Belgium's neutral status.

Approved as early as 1904, the Schlieffen Plan, whereby Germany would attack France via Belgium, was implemented on August 4, 1914. Unprepared for an invasion, Belgium quickly lost control over all of her assets. Having devoted the prewar years to becoming an industrial power, Belgium was one of the world's most industrialised nations by 1914, with one of the densest networks of road and rail transport in Europe. To gain and maintain their control over Belgium, the Germans quickly destroyed most of her heavy industry.

The end of World War I in Europe in 1918 ended German control of Belgium. The Conference of Versailles met between 1918 and 1919 and issued the peace treaty that formally concluded the war. Belgium was restored to its status as an independent country and was given BF 2 million to counteract the devastation that the Germans had inflicted during their four-year occupation. This sum covered less than one-third of the damage that had occurred in 1915 alone.

After World War I, Belgium returned to her previous policy of neutrality. The interwar years were spent rebuilding damaged sections and restoring the economy to its prewar status. The determination of her people enabled Belgium to rise from ruins after World War I and return to rapid industrialisation, resulting in Belgium's becoming the most densely populated country in Europe after the war.

Restored to its antebellum status, Belgium's industry, transport and economy continued to flourish, despite ongoing conflict over the official language. Divided into two sections, Belgium comprises the Flemish-speaking people of Flanders, the northern section, and the French-speaking population in Wallonia, the southern section. Debates concerning the language factor persist today, yet they have never overshadowed the determination of an entire country to rise to a position of power and status in Europe—a position that was undermined by the Germans again in World War II.

Without issuing a formal declaration of war, the Germans invaded Belgium on May 10, 1940, a tactic dictated, as before, by Belgium's location vis-á-vis France. Almost immediately, the Germans established control over Belgium's border territories and

Opposite: This Brussels department store, L'Innovation, is a classic example of mature Art Nouveau architecture and is considered one of Victor Horta's finest designs. The building was constructed of iron, glass and granite, with a vaulted central bay, in 1901; it was destroyed in 1966–67.

destroyed more than half of her air force. After the bombing of the great port of Rotterdam on May 15—the first example of the destruction of ancient and populous cities that would be characteristic of the conflict—King Leopold III surrendered and became a prisoner of war. The Belgian army quickly followed suit, surrendering to the Germans on May 28. Their control over Belgium, officially acknowledged by the country, enabled the Germans to exert their influence over all aspects of life and living conditions. Strict economic control was exercised, and harsh rationing measures were enacted.

However, the Belgian Congo (later known as Zaire, and in 1997 renamed the Republic of Congo) remained outside of the Germans' control, and the African colony assisted the Allied war effort through donations of her gold reserves. Between 1940 and 1943, the Belgian Congo contributed more than $US 28.5 million to the war effort, enabling the Allies to continue fighting. The money donated by the Belgian Congo also helped to reconstruct countries that had been damaged by the war and paid in full Belgium's expenses for repairing the damages inflicted by the Germans during the most horrific war of the twentieth century.

The Allies liberated Belgium in September 1944, and efforts to undo the architectural and economic devastation inflicted by the Germans commenced. The challenge was a daunting one. Among the most significant architectural losses were: the seventeenth-century Town Hall and late Gothic (1520) Church of St. Catherine in Hoogstraten (both completely demolished); the Convent of the Beguines in Aerschot, 1170 (severely damaged); the Church of St. Gertrude, Nivelles, 1046 (severely damaged); and many medieval structures in Tournai, whose wartime devastation is featured in the plates following these pages.

Faced again with the destruction caused by world war, the government re-evaluated Belgium's neutral status—a position that was abandoned in favor of a strong mili-

tary and political alliance system and an active foreign policy. The years of Belgium's traditional neutrality were over.

Together with Great Britain, France, the Netherlands and Luxembourg, Belgium concluded the Treaty of Brussels in 1948. This treaty guaranteed a fifty-year alliance against armed attack. A year later, in 1949, the North Atlantic Treaty Organization (NATO) was created in order to include North America in Western Europe's alliance. NATO was such a successful organisation that it was joined by Greece and Turkey (1952), Western Germany (1955) and Spain (1982). Belgium's new position in world affairs was manifested by the selection of Brussels as NATO headquarters.

Belgium also played a leading role in the formation of the United Nations (UN), becoming one of the organisation's founding members in 1945. Paul Henri Spaak, Belgium's prime minister in 1938–9 and 1947–50, became the first president of the UN's General Assembly.

Due to the strength of her alliances and the determination of her leaders, Belgium has managed to avoid renewed involvement in international conflicts. Her role has been to join other countries to ensure that such conflicts never occur again. As a result, Belgium was able to rectify most of the damage inflicted on her towns, villages and people during both World Wars. However, Belgium has not been spared from all destruction. In late 1984, Brussels and Antwerp were bombed by terrorists attempting to destroy NATO's defense supplies, proving that Belgium's revocation of her traditional neutrality would both create and resolve issues of military and tactical destruction. In common with other European countries, too, industrial and infrastructure modernisation and commercial pressures have led to the demolition of some significant buildings, but Belgium's conservationist movement has been highly successful in restricting such losses as well as in its restoration initiatives.

—Anke van Zanten

Hôtel Aubecq, Brussels *Above*
Victor Horta (1861–1947) was an internationally
renowned architect whose 1892 design for the Brussels
home of Professor Tassel was the first example of Art
Nouveau architecture. Combining elements of the
English Arts and Crafts Movement, the innovative
ironwork of Eugène Emmanuel Viollet-le-Duc and
traditional French floral motifs and organic shapes, his
work was a major influence on Hector Guimard, who
designed the famous Paris Métro entrances. Unlike
many of Horta's buildings, The Hôtel Aubecq, 1900
(demolished), was constructed almost entirely of
stone, with little ironwork. In addition to this and
L'Innovation (see page 76), his House of the People
(Brussels, 1896–1900) was also demolished—
an indication that Belgium's conservation efforts have
been directed primarily toward architecture that
predated the modern period.

World War II Destruction in Tournai *Following Pages*
Four before-and-after views of the bomb-ravaged city
of Tournai: the Grand Place; the Pont aux Pommes;
the Rue des Maux; and the railway station. The city
was rich in medieval buildings and monuments as
well as structures from the era of Louis XIV, whose
rule commenced in 1667. Whole sections of the old
town were destroyed in the bombing, although,
remarkably, the cathedral, shown standing behind
the devastation of the Grand Place on the next page,
survived virtually intact.

Germany

Until the outbreak of World War II, Germany luxuriated in an impressive architectural heritage that incorporated a rich variety of styles, including Romanesque, Gothic, Neoclassical, *Rundbogenstil* (round-arched style) and the more recent Bauhaus designs. Hitler's invasion of Poland, however, imperilled the country's architectural gems and, as many cities were relentlessly bombed by the Allies, a large number of significant buildings were punished for the *Führer*'s aggressive ambitions.

Apart from a few isolated examples of buildings ravaged by natural causes, such as the fire that swept through Hamburg in 1842, Germany's architectural inheritance had survived relatively unscathed until 1943. The only real threat that it faced was that of urban aggrandisement: Berlin, for example, underwent an extensive building programme under the supervision of the Prussian architect Karl Friedrich von Schinkel (1781–1841), whose Neoclassical vision was, in turn, menaced by the megalomaniacal plans of Hitler and his architect Albert Speer (1905–81). Fortunately, in the latter case, only the new *Reichskanzlei* (Reich Chancellory) had been completed by 1939 (it was destroyed during the following decade), when war brought a halt to Hitler's radical plans to rebuild Berlin completely as the grandiose "Germania." During the early years of the twentieth century, new styles of architecture, such as *Jugendstil* (Art Nouveau), Functionalism and Expressionism, had flourished. However, Hitler disapproved of these "decadent" styles and favoured the uninspiring and monumental works of Paul Ludwig Troost and Speer. Had war not intervened, Hitler (who fancied himself as

an architect) might have obliterated architectural innovation altogether; as it was, many notable modern structures in Germany's industrialised north were destroyed by Allied bombs.

During the early years of the war, direct fighting was confined to Germany's periphery, but in 1943 a new and terrible form of warfare was unleashed on the country: saturation bombing. Until 1940 the bombing of Germany had been strictly limited to legitimate military targets; in May of that year, British prime minister Winston Churchill decided that bombardment should extend to industrial and other areas in order both to destroy Germany's industrial capacity and to demoralise its citizens. The Battle of Britain caused this policy to be shelved temporarily. After this brief respite, in 1942, Air Marshal Arthur T. Harris was made head of the British Bomber Command and given the order: "The main goal of attack should from now on be the morale of the enemy population." Accordingly, the U.S. Eighth Air Force and Britain's Bomber Command instituted Operation Pointblank, a round-the-clock aerial offensive carried out from British airbases. While the Americans operated during the daylight hours, concentrating on such tactical targets as industrial installations, oil refineries and transport networks, British pilots were responsible for "carpet-bombing" key German cities at night, when anti-aircraft resistance was lowest. As the war drew on, the scale of the bombing raids was stepped up, and from August 1944 until the end of the war, it is estimated that as many as 127 German cities were attacked on 194 days and 94 nights.

The bombers wreaked terrible destruction: on May 30–31, 1942, Köln (Cologne) was devastated by 1,046 bombers whose

Opposite: *A prewar photograph of the medieval architecture on Nikolaifleet, Hamburg, with the spire of St. Nikolaikirche (pictured on page 88) rising behind the centre building.*

payloads unleashed uncontrollable, tornadolike firestorms. Although the famous cathedral miraculously survived, large numbers of this Catholic city's churches were damaged. Hamburg, which was subjected to mass-bombing assaults in July 1943, lost nearly 300,000 buildings (as well as 30,000 citizens) to the Allied bombs and subsequent firestorms. Lübeck, Essen, Königsberg, Magdeburg, Chemnitz, Pforzheim, Dessau, Dortmund, Nürnberg, Würzburg, Kiel, München (Munich), Pilsen and Leipzig—all these cities, and many more, were targeted, and paid a dreadful price for the aspirations of the *Führer*. The bombing of Dresden in February 1945 was particularly controversial: the city was crowded with refugees from the east, and estimates of the dead range from 60,000 to 245,000. Most of this beautiful city was destroyed. As Germany's capital and the nerve centre of government, Berlin was bombed almost constantly from 1943 until the end of the war, and suffered further during the Battle of Berlin, which culminated in the Soviets' advance to its centre. One cannot quantify human suffering, but the statistics give some idea of the scale of the architectural devastation: of Frankfurt-am-Main's estimated 44,559 buildings, for example, only 8,683 survived. During the last year of the war, further destruction was inflicted, particularly on eastern Germany, where the Red Army left a smoking trail of fired buildings in their wake.

At the end of the war, the defeated Germany found itself standing at *Stunde null* (zero hour). Now a divided country occupied by the Allies, its cities lay in ruins, and there was little wherewithal with which to rebuild them. Armies of *Trümmerfrauen* ("rubble women") were recruited to sort through the rubble, both to restore some semblance of order, and to retrieve valuable building materials for recycling. A few essential structures were hurriedly erected, but there was no systematic town planning—at this point, little could be done. It was only after the currency was reformed in 1948 and West Germany began to receive American Marshall Aid, from 1949, that the economy recovered sufficiently even to contemplate a rebuilding programme. Yet, from the 1950s, thanks partly to American aid, partly to Ludwig Erhard's *soziale Marktwirtschaft* (social-market economy), and partly to their own determination and industriousness, the West Germans achieved a *Wirtschaftswunder* (economic miracle). At last it was possible to start to reconstruct the shattered towns.

From the 1950s, therefore, rebuilding was carried out with a vengeance. Many cities, including Hamburg and Frankfurt-am-Main, had been so devastated that there was no alternative to rebuilding them in a largely modern, international style. Yet every effort was made to restore meticulously and, if necessary, even to reconstruct those buildings and areas that had been of special importance, and, as a result, most West German towns today boast at the very least an historically authentic *Rathaus* (town hall) and some key churches, whose modern incarnation scarcely differs from their prewar appearance. Modern extensions have been imaginatively attached to the shells of some ecclesiastical buildings that were beyond repair: the most celebrated example is the Kaiser-Wilhelm-Gedächtnis-Kirche in Berlin, to whose blackened stump Egon Eiermann (1904–70) added an octagonal church and bell tower between 1955 and 1963. This church is now a memorial to the victims of war and of Nazism; other, similar examples include Köln's St. Albans and Hamburg's St. Nikolai.

After 1945 Germany was partitioned, and many of its fine old cities were ceded to other nations, including Danzig (which became Poland's Gdansk), and Königsberg (which became the Soviet Kaliningrad). What remained of eastern Germany, including that part of Berlin that contained the most architecturally significant buildings, declined under Soviet control; in East Berlin, those monuments that were considered "reactionary and militaristic," such as Kaiser Wilhelm's mounted statue, were torn down. The Hohenzollern *Schloß* (castle), which, although war-damaged, could have been restored, was demolished in 1950, as a sign of the Communist government's determination to reject the old order, and the *Palast der Republik* (Palace of the Republic) was erected in its place (ironically, it was closed in 1990 due to asbestos contamination). Soviet revenge on the country that had inflicted so much suffering on its own citizens was merciless: those parts of East Germany's industry that had survived the war were removed to the Soviet Union. Until 1960, therefore, rebuilding was slow—and those new buildings that were erected displayed the features of the politically appropriate "socialist realism" style.

From about the late 1950s, however, East Germany finally found itself in a position to begin restoring certain major buildings in cities like East Berlin, Leipzig, Dresden, Frankfurt-an-der-Oder and Karl-Marx-Stadt (Chemnitz). As in West Germany, work was carried out to a historically exacting standard, and impressive examples of reconstructed edifices include the Leipzig Opera House (reopened in 1960) and Dresden's Semper Opera House (1985).

In November 1989 the Berlin Wall, which had divided the city for so long, was opened, heralding German reunification. Since then, despite the huge cost, even greater effort has gone into restoring eastern Germany's important buildings, including Dresden's ruined Frauenkirche, which had served as a harrowing reminder of the tragedy of war for decades.

Unlike many other nationalities who perhaps take their architectural history for granted, Germans lost so many buildings of historical importance during World War II that they have a profound appreciation of their architectural heritage, and are actively determined to preserve what remains. Although Germany still bears the deep scars that resulted from Hitler's policies—in both architectural and general terms—many glorious civic, ecclesiastical and cultural monuments remain, serving both as a testimony to the vision of their architects and builders, and as a sign of German pride in its buildings. Thus, although new construction is taking place constantly, there is little danger that buildings of architectural significance will be razed to make space for modern structures.
— CLARA BRENGER

Left: A 1908 photograph of Munich's Karlsplatz, laid out by Karl Theodor in 1791. The Karlstor (centre), built in 1315, once formed part of the city walls. The Rondel buildings on each side of the gate were erected between 1796 and 1802 and modernised a century later; although they suffered bomb damage during World War II, they have since been restored. In the background are the twin towers of the Frauenkirche (Church of Our Lady), also severely bomb damaged but subsequently restored.

St. Nikolaikirche, Hamburg *Opposite*
Hamburg attained prosperity during the Middle
Ages through sea trade. By 1913 it was the world's
third-largest port, and its industrial and strategic
importance made it a prime target for Allied bombing.
In July 1943 air raids devastated the city, killing tens
of thousands.

One of Hamburg's many notable buildings was the
neo-Gothic St. Nikolaikirche (Church of St. Nicholas),
built between 1845–63 by the English architect Sir
George Gilbert Scott (1811–78) to replace a medieval
church that had been consumed by fire in 1842.
The new St. Nikolaikirche was largely destroyed in a
bombing raid in 1943. Today only its spire remains.

The Uhlenhorst Fährhaus, Hamburg *Above*
At Hamburg's centre lies a lake, the Alster, which is
divided by a bridge into the small Binnenalster and
the larger Außenalster. The Uhlenhorst Fährhaus (a
ferry house), situated on the banks of one of the canals
leading off the Außenalster, was not only a landing
stage but a vibrant place of entertainment,
incorporating a large café garden and a popular dance
venue. Although many of the solid merchants' villas
around the Alster escaped destruction during World
War II, the Uhlenhorst Fährhaus was destroyed and
was not rebuilt.

Altdeutsches Haus and Knochenhauerhaus, Hildesheim *Opposite and above*
The Ottonian town of Hildesheim in Lower Saxony was virtually razed to the ground by
Allied bombers during World War II. Much of the town has since been rebuilt in an
uninspiring, modern style, but some notable buildings, including the *Dom* (cathedral)
and the Knochenhauerhaus (butchers' guildhall) have been meticulously reconstructed.
The Knochenhauerhaus, above, dates from 1529 and is distinguished by its fine, half-
timbered frame and carvings. The Altdeutsches Haus (Old German House), opposite,
c.1600, was completely destroyed and has not been rebuilt.

Köln Before and After Air Raids *Opposite and above*
During World War II, the prosperous Rhineland city
of Köln (Cologne) was one of the first targets for the
Allied "thousand-bomber" raids: on the night of May
30–31, 1942, Allied bombs transformed the city into a
blazing inferno. This was not the last such raid on the
city: it was bombed almost continually until the end of
the war. As a result of these aerial attacks, it was
estimated that 90 percent of the inner city was
destroyed, along with 70 percent of the outlying areas.
Despite suffering fourteen direct hits, however, the
huge, twin-spired Gothic cathedral that dominates
Köln's skyline emerged relatively unscathed, but a large
number of this predominantly Catholic city's churches
were damaged beyond restoration. Many of Köln's old
buildings, such as the churches of St. Maria im Kapitol
and Groß St. Martin, or such houses as those on the
Neumarkt or the Overstolzenhaus, have since been
painstakingly restored. Given the overwhelming extent
of the bomb damage inflicted during World War II,
however, it is perhaps inevitable that much of present-
day Köln's architecture dates from the postwar period.

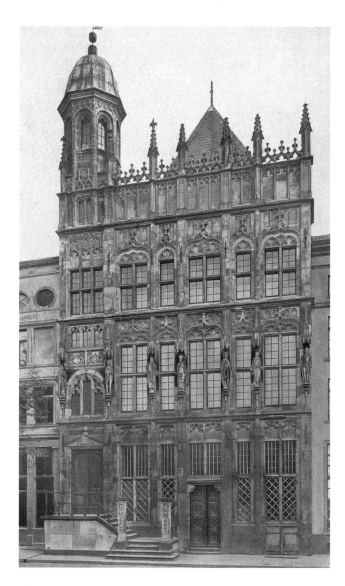

Pellerhaus, Nürnberg *Left*

The Bavarian city of Nürnberg (Nuremberg) was perceived as the symbolic seat of Nazism, and an estimated 90 percent of the city was destroyed by Allied bombers. Jakob Wolff the Elder's famous Pellerhaus (Egidienplatz No.3), a patrician house built between 1602 and 1605 for B. Viatis, was badly damaged in October 1944 and then gutted by fire in January 1945. It was rebuilt in 1956–57 to a predominantly modern design, retaining only the arches on the ground level and some of the surviving façade of the courtyard gallery. Today it serves as a state archive and town library.

Town Hall, Wesel *Right*

The Ruhr city of Wesel was bombed to rubble during 1945, and of all the buildings lining the Großen Markt (large market), only the Willibrordikirche (St. Willibrord's Church) could be restored. Among the architectural treasures that were lost was the *Rathaus* (town hall), a three-storey structure on the Großen Markt built between 1390 and 1396, whose sandstone façade dated from 1455–56.

The Markt, *Mainz* *Above*

The barrows, baskets and multitude of stores in this early photograph of the *Markt* (market) give an indication of its status as Mainz's lively heart. On one day—February 27, 1945—however, British bombers flattened 85 percent of the inner city, including the *Markt*. During the following decades, the citizens carefully restored many of the old buildings, lovingly recreating the original façades of the sixteenth-, seventeenth- and eighteenth-century houses on the *Markt,* as well as the adjacent *Dom* (cathedral). The Renaissance *Marktbrunnen* (market fountain) has similarly been restored and brightly painted.

Kaiser-Wilhelm-Gedächtniskirche, Berlin *Opposite*
Erected between 1891 and 1895 in memory of Kaiser
(emperor) Wilhelm I: Allied bombing devastated the
neo-Romanesque Kaiser-Wilhelm-Gedächtniskirche
(Kaiser Wilhelm Memorial Church), truncating
its spire in the process. Today the ruined church
incorporates a memorial to the victims of war and
is a symbol of Berlin. A hexagonal bell tower and
octagonal church of concrete and blue glass were built
between 1955 and 1963 by Egon Eiermann (1904–70)
next to the preserved ruins. Many critics consider
the postwar reconstruction an improvement on the
original building.

Leipzigerstraße, Berlin *Above*
The prewar Leipzigerstraße was one of Berlin's premier
shopping streets and traffic routes, whose many
famous attractions included Frederick the Great's
Royal Berlin porcelain factory; the monumental
Wertheim department store of 1906 (designed by
Alfred Messel, featuring innovative plate-glass
windows); and Kempinski's restaurant, which was re-
established by its Jewish owners after the war on the
Kurfürstendamm. Many notable, albeit damaged,
buildings were razed to the ground in 1961 to create a
no-man's-land area behind the Berlin Wall. In 1969 the
East German government began to reconstruct the
Leipzigerstraße, erecting ugly and repetitive apartment
buildings as a defiant demonstration of socialist
planning. Today it is again a busy shopping street, but
its erstwhile unique character has been forever lost.

Alexanderplatz, Berlin *Left*

Before World War II, Alexanderplatz, created by Frederick the Great in 1778 and later named in honour of the tsar who visited Berlin in 1805, was a bustling square. After suffering damage from prolonged Allied bombing and the Soviets' battle for Berlin, it became part of the eastern sector of the city. In November 1989 it was the site of an historic demonstration that heralded the opening of the Berlin Wall, yet it presented a sad contrast to the vitality of the square once described by the novelist Arthur Döblin, in *Berlin Alexanderplatz,* as "the quivering heart of a cosmopolitan city." Now surrounded by high, precast-concrete 1960s buildings, Alexanderplatz appears drab and soulless, its few distinguishing features including the *Weltzeituhr* (world time clock), and the *Fernsehturm* (television tower), which towers over the thirteenth-century Marienkirche (St. Mary's Church). It remains a busy traffic junction and commercial area.

Schloßplatz, Berlin Left

Dating from the fifteenth century, the *Schloß* (castle), on the right of this 1905 picture, survived severe bomb damage but was destroyed on September 7, 1950, as a symbol of East Germany's renunciation of the old Prussian values (it had once been the residence of the Hohenzollern dynasty). The Schloßplatz/Lustgarten (pleasure garden) area was renamed Marx-Engels-Platz, and a new parliament building was erected on the site. The doorway ('Portal IV') and balcony from which the Spartakist leader Karl Liebknecht had declared a "free socialist republic" in November 1918, was saved. After reunification in 1990, the parliament building had to be closed down because of asbestos contamination. The *Dom* (cathedral), on the left, was built between 1894 and 1905 by Julius Raschdorf on the site of Frederick the Great's 1750 cathedral. Damaged during World War II, it has only recently undergone extensive restoration.

Potsdamerplatz, Berlin Above

Potsdamerplatz was once one of Europe's busiest squares. In the rear centre of the photograph can be seen one of Schinkel's twin Potsdam gates; the large building left of centre is the Palast Hotel, and that on the far right the Hotel der Fürstenhof. The devastating Allied bombing and Soviet onslaught flattened Potsdamerplatz, although the steel skeleton of the Columbushaus (see page 105) survived. After 1945, Potsdamerplatz found itself in the Soviet sector, directly on the border between East and West Berlin. In 1956 the remains of the Columbushaus and the Potsdam gates were meticulously destroyed to make way for the Berlin Wall and its death-strip. Today Potsdamerplatz remains bleak, but a rebuilding programme is under way. As West Berlin's mayor, Walter Momper, stated in 1989 as he crossed from East to West, "This is where the old heart of Berlin used to beat, and it will beat again."

War Damage in Dresden *These pages and overleaf*
Before the fateful night of February 13–14, 1945, the
Baroque "Florence on the Elbe" was universally
considered one of Europe's loveliest cities. Much of
Dresden's splendid architecture was commissioned by
Augustus II "the Strong" (1670–1733), to glorify the city
in accordance with his status as elector of Saxony and
king of Poland. The bombing of the refugee-packed
city at such a late stage in the war was one of the most
controversial Allied decisions of World War II. Three-
quarters of the city was destroyed. Among the
magnificent buildings that were severely damaged
were the domed Frauenkirche (built between 1726 and
1743) and the 1547 Residenzschloß (castle). The
Kreuzkirche (Church of the Cross) on the *Altmarkt*
(Old Market), shown on the next page, was gutted but

still standing after the raid. The dignified buildings of
Dresden's Prager Straße, shown on the following page
in before-and-after views from the *Hauptbahnhof*
(main station), were replaced after the war by
modern concrete buildings. Today it is a busy
pedestrian shopping street and a bustling centre of the
consumer culture.

After the war, Dresden became part of East
Germany; there was little money to spare for its
reconstruction, and rebuilding was generally in a
utilitarian style. A few important showpieces, however,
such as the Baroque Zwinger complex, and the
Renaissance-style Semper Opera House, which was
reopened in 1985, were faithfully, if slowly, restored.
Since German reunification, the reconstruction effort
has gained new momentum.

Erich Mendelsohn Masterpieces *Opposite and above*
Despite Germany's conservation efforts, some
architecturally significant buildings have been lost
since the war. A leading Expressionist and Modernist
architect, Erich Mendelsohn (1867–1953) designed
adventurous, supremely functional buildings,
including the 1926 Schocken department store in
Stuttgart (demolished in a 1955 urban-renewal and
town-planning scheme) and the streamlined

Columbushaus, above, on Berlin's Potsdamerplatz
(pulled down in 1956). He utilised the new building
materials of glass, steel and concrete to stunning
effect, heralding the geometric, Modernist style. The
Hermann Hat Factory at Luckenwalde, opposite below
(demolished), was built in 1923 for Friedrich Steinberg
of Hermann & Co., to house the company's dye vats.
A multi-angled roof and the hatblock motif made the
building distinctive.

Italy

Italy has an unrivalled architectural heritage stretching back over 2,000 years. Some of the greatest architects of all time — Bramante, Michelangelo, Bernini and Palladio — created styles that were emulated throughout the world. The ancient builders of the Roman Empire left behind buildings of such perfect proportions that their work dominated architectural convention for centuries. As the centre of the Christian world, Italian ecclesiastical architecture reaches its apogee at St. Peter's in Rome. Although subject to forces for architectural change that apply throughout the world, succeeding generations of Italians have preserved and restored the buildings of their ancestors.

The first lost city of Italy is Pompeii, a town whose demise in AD 79 was recorded so graphically by Pliny the Younger that his report seems as immediate as those recording the fire in Venice's La Fenice Theatre in 1996. It is impossible to recover from the kind of destruction wreaked by the volcano of Mount Vesuvius, but a new town emerged next to the ancient city. Today it is a shadow of its ancient namesake, little more than a rather tatty suburb of Naples. The ruins of ancient Pompeii, however, are one of the great archaeological wonders of the world, despite the depredations of overly zealous eighteenth-century historians and the march of time.

Successive Italian governments have ensured that the works of great architects were preserved: they have devoted many billions of lira to such projects. It is also worth remembering that many of Italy's greatest buildings — those of the Renaissance — were constructed at a time when the country was invaded and fought over by a long succession of foreign armies.

Incredibly, out of this chaos rose the graceful towers of San Gimignano, the palaces of Florence and Venice and some of the great buildings of Rome — the works of Bramante and Michelangelo. Fortunately, the will to preserve these splendid buildings has been almost as strong as the great egos that commissioned them.

Few people are more aware of their ancient buildings and monuments than are the Italians. However, the preservation and restoration of this magnificent architectural heritage has never been a straightforward task, and difficult decisions have been necessary. Mussolini, for example, has been rightly praised for clearing the medieval tenements that clung to the sides of many ancient Roman monuments, including Trajan's Column, and for his foresight in widening some of the city streets to provide for automotive traffic. In so doing, however, he destroyed some of Rome's medieval heritage. Similarly, after World War II, the whole of Italy was faced with the massive rebuilding task that also confronted several other European countries. The country was suffering an acute financial crisis: industrial fixtures had been destroyed, thousands of acres of agricultural land lay fallow and there was a severe housing shortage. City planners with limited budgets faced the unenviable choice of restoring old buildings, or erecting new ones to house the war-weary masses.

Certain factors govern architectural change everywhere: disasters, both natural and manmade, demographic shifts and the impact of economic factors including industrialisation, tourism and commerce. Italy has suffered a number of earthquakes, volcanic eruptions and floods. Venice is slowly sinking into the Adriatic Sea, but a

Opposite: Regarded as one of Palladio's masterpieces, the Palazzo Valmarana at Vicenza was constructed c. 1566 for Leonardo Valmarana. The exterior of the villa was simple, and ornamentation was confined to the windows and doors, while the triple-arched entrance opened into a vaulted interior reminiscent of the ancient Roman baths. The structure was heavily damaged during World War II.

Above: *A detail of the bronze doors of the Cathedral at Benevento, believed to be the work of Greek artists during the twelfth and thirteenth centuries. The cathedral was almost entirely destroyed during World War II (see pages 116–17).*

an end to the comparative peace enjoyed by the Italian population until then. The advance north was achieved as a result of bitter fighting. The monastery of Monte Cassino, south of Rome, was probably the most famous casualty, but most of Salerno and parts of Naples were also destroyed. The medieval cathedral of Benevento was bombed, and only the campanile survives. As the Germans retreated from Florence, they blew up every bridge apart from the Ponte Vecchio. Happily, Rome emerged almost intact: only one church, San Francesco di Paolo, suffered damage.

Fortunately, Allied forces involved in the invasion included officers assigned to the newly created subcommission on Monuments, Fine Arts and Archives. Their mandate was to avoid as much damage as possible by briefing ground and air forces on the location of significant buildings and sites. When such buildings were damaged, these officers worked closely with Italian museum and fine arts personnel to render "first aid." Extensive reconstruction was carried out in the postwar years.

The nineteenth century was not a glorious era for Italian architecture, rather, a rare period when Italian architectural styles failed to dominate European taste. The prevailing fashion was for the overblown Beaux-Arts styles emanating from France. It was during this period, however, that a great many medieval buildings were restored, prompted perhaps by the feelings of nationalism produced by Garibaldi and the *Risorgimento*. Architects took great care to replicate medieval craftsmanship as closely as possible, and as a result the medieval centres of such cities as Florence, Venice and Siena appear much as they did five hundred years ago.

Italy's architectural heritage, the fountainhead of magnificent buildings all over Europe, is second to none. During the past fifty years, new construction has proceeded hand in hand with conservation and restoration activities.

— Mila Riggio

vigorous conservation campaign ensures that the city's buildings are preserved. Ironically, the most recent loss has been due to fire, when the La Fenice (Phoenix) Theatre was gutted early in 1996. The Arno flooded Florence in 1966, damaging many artistic treasures in the Uffizi, but leaving some of the city's loveliest buildings relatively unscathed.

In twentieth-century Italy, war has been the primary cause of the destruction of great architectural monuments. It was not until 1943 that significant war damage occurred. The occupying Germans tried to prevent unnecessary destruction to Italy's wealth of artistic treasures by shipping many items back to Gestapo headquarters in Berlin. The onslaught of the Allied invasions, launched from Salerno in 1943, meant

La Fenice, Venice *Below*

Teatro La Fenice (Phoenix Theatre), the principal opera house in Venice, was badly damaged by fire in February 1996. Built in 1790–92 at the expense of the Nobile Societá, a group of wealthy merchants and citizens, and designed by the architect Gian Antonio Selva, La Fenice has survived two major fires, the first having occurred in 1836.

Termini Station, Rome   *Above*
Completed in 1876, when large tracts of Rome were
being rebuilt for the city's role as capital of the recently
unified Italy, Termini Station was characteristic of
the nation's Neoclassical architecture. This florid,
cathedral-like edifice was replaced by a structure of
concrete, glass and steel after Mussolini decreed a
competition to replace the original building in 1937.
The modern structure was completed in 1950.

The Borgo, Rome *Above*

This photograph of St. Peter's Basilica and the surrounding area includes the medieval neighbourhood known as the Borgo (above the circular courtyard), a labyrinth of narrow streets and picturesque houses. Mussolini demolished this area in 1934–7 to make way for the Via della Conciliazione, a wide avenue leading from the River Tiber to St. Peter's. It was constructed to celebrate a major achievement of the Fascist régime: the Lateran Treaty of 1929, which ended the eighty-year division between Church and state. Among the historical houses lost was Raphael's studio, which had survived intact for some four hundred years.

Church of San Lorenzo Fuori le Mura, Rome   *Above*
The ancient Church of San Lorenzo combines two
structures. The first was founded by Constantine in
330 on the site of a small domestic shrine to St.
Lawrence, later replaced with a basilica during the
pontificate of Pelagius III; the second, dedicated to the
Virgin Mary, was built late in the eighth century. In
1943 San Lorenzo was hit by a bomb intended for a
nearby railway marshalling yard, and the western
façade, with the portico constructed by Pope Honorius
III between 1216 and 1227, was destroyed.

Central Railway Station, Milan *Above*
Designed by Bouchot, Milan's Central Railway Station
was constructed between 1857 and 1864 in the popular
and flamboyant French Beaux-Arts style. It is
characteristic of the mid-nineteenth century, when
Italy followed rather than led architectural trends. Like
so many grandiose terminals of the day, it succumbed
to "modernisation." Some Milanese buildings,
including the Marino Palace, Santa Maria delle Grazie
and San Ambrogio, suffered damage during World War
II, but the city centre has survived the century
relatively unscathed.

The Towers, Bologna *Opposite, above*
Referred to today as the "Two Towers," Bologna
originally boasted four towers, as shown in this
photograph from the mid–1910s. The two shortened
towers in the foreground, Artemesia and Riccadonna,
were demolished when Bologna underwent a drastic
process of urban renewal. During this period, avenues
were cut through the historical centre of the city and
wide areas of "unattractive" housing were cleared to
make way for more impressive and monumental
squares. Only the Torre degli Asinelli (centre right)
and La Garisenda (centre left) exist today.

Porticoes, Bologna *Below*
Bologna is famous for its porticoes, more numerous
than those of any comparable city. They testify to
Bologna's long history as a powerful city-state that
came under papal rule in 1506. In 1939 this historic
portico was demolished to make way for a *Casa del
Fascio* (a Fascist Party headquarters), which, due to the
onset of World War II, was never built. After the war
the state telephone company erected an unremarkable
office building on the site.

Benevento Cathedral, Benevento *Opposite and Above*
Benevento Cathedral was created by combining
fragments of Roman and Lombard architecture into
a Christian church, in what was described as a true
meeting of secular and religious design. Originally
constructed in the eleventh century, the cathedral
was enlarged during Cardinal Ruggiero's jurisdiction
(1179–1221). These before-and-after pictures show the
damage inflicted by the Allied invasion in 1943. Only
the thirteenth-century campanile survived.

The Republics of Former Yugoslavia

Buildings, places of worship, monuments and old ruins have served an important role in the cultures of all ethnic groups in former Yugoslavia. They have stood as reminders of historic events, struggles and the perseverance that brought ethnic Slavic tribes into the Balkan region in the sixth century AD and secured their presence, culture and traditions in the area for centuries to come. Historic buildings and ancient structures continue to provide the ethnic populace of former Yugoslavia with a sense of belonging, reaffirming their rightful ownership of lands where their ancestors lived and died through centuries of battles, hardship and prosperity.

In the medieval period, territories comprising future Yugoslavia were the setting for relentless warfare between ethnic kingdoms and competing empires. In the seventeenth, eighteenth and early nineteenth centuries, areas of Croatia and northern Serbia were dominated by the Austro-Hungarian Empire, while Serbia proper—Bosnia-Hercegovina, Montenegro and Macedonia—comprised various kingdoms and dukedoms that struggled against persistent onslaught and domination by the Ottoman Empire.

"Yugoslavia: Kingdom of Serbs, Croats and Slovenes" was created in 1917 by King Alexander, who united these and other ethnic groups within one "south Slavic" state, as its name indicates. During World War II, the country was torn apart by civil war. In 1945 the Yugoslav Partisan Resistance Movement, headed by Marshal Josip Broz Tito, consolidated and reorganized Yugoslavia by creating six republics: Serbia, Croatia, Bosnia-Hercegovina, Macedonia, Slovenia and Montenegro. This structure remained until 1991, when the country began to break apart due to civil strife.

Remains of some of the oldest structures in former Yugoslavia can be found primarily in Serbian areas that had been inhabited by various ethnic groups and empires since before the birth of Christ. Although centuries of neglect and destruction from countless battles have taken their toll on these ancient structures, the greatest amount of destruction and damage has occurred during the twentieth century. The façades of many Yugoslav buildings were greatly damaged during World War II, especially in the capital, Belgrade, which experienced extensive bombing and shelling. The tragic Yugoslav civil war of the 1990s was particularly devastating to buildings and monuments in Bosnia-Hercegovina as a result of the fighting among the three major ethnic groups, the Bosnian Serbs, Croats and Muslims.

Belgrade, the capital of Serbia, is the oldest city in former Yugoslavia. The old fortified city was nestled on the confluence of two rivers: the Danube and the Sava. No other city in former Yugoslavia has had as many battles fought around it, nor as much turnover of occupying powers. The scars on Belgrade's ancient city walls attest to centuries of warfare, during which the city was overtaken by a number of competing powers, anxious to control Belgrade's excellent strategic position between Central and Eastern Europe.

Belgrade was inhabited as early as the third century BC by the Celts, who built a fortress on the grounds of the city they

Opposite: The Stari Most bridge spanning the Neretva River in Mostar was built under the rule of Suleyman the Magnificent in 1566. It linked the city's ethnic quarters, joining Muslims, Croats and Serbs. It was destroyed in November 1993 and has become a tragic symbol of the region's civil war.

named "Singidinum." In the first and second centuries BC, the conquering Romans rebuilt the fortified city in a typically Roman rectangular design, serving an important strategic role at the time. In the fifth and sixth centuries AD, the city walls were attacked often, by the Huns, Goths, Avars and Slavic tribes from the north. The city was renamed "Bjelgrad" in the year 878, when it was taken over by conquering Slavic tribes, mostly the Serbs. During the Middle Ages, the city was fought over and intermittently controlled by the Bulgarians, Serbs and Hungarians.

Following years of Turkish onslaught during the fourteenth century on areas of southern Serbia, Serbia's Tsar Dusan moved north and established the fortress city of Belgrade as his capital. But after Dusan's death in 1355, the city fell to the Hungarians. Following extensive battles in the fourteenth and fifteenth centuries, Belgrade changed ownership several times between the Hungarians and Serbs, after which the city fell to the Turks in 1521. Austrians ruled the city toward the end of the seventeenth century, having defeated the Turks in 1682. Following a number of uprisings, in 1806 the Serbian population regained control of the city, which has continued to be pre-dominantly populated and controlled by the Serbs up until the present day.

Belgrade's architecture and buildings suffered considerable damage in 1914 and 1915 due to Austrian and German attacks during World War I; German attacks did further damage in World War II. Many old buildings in Belgrade have been renovated during the past ten years. Cobblestones from the seventeenth century still pave parts of the old city. Although the old fortress towers have been largely destroyed over the centuries, an extensive network of fortress walls, medieval towers and monasteries still overlooks the Danube and Sava Rivers.

Zagreb, the capital of Croatia, did not become a significantly large city until the eleventh century. For this reason, it was spared some of the pre-medieval and medieval-period attacks experienced by Belgrade. Zagreb was also protected from attacks by the Ottoman Empire, since most of Croatia, as well as Slovenia, gained independence and autonomy after World War I with the establishment of Yugoslavia in 1917. Today Zagreb is made up of an upper part comprising the old city and a lower, more modern, part that stretches toward the River Sava.

Montenegro did not become a separately controlled territory until the fourteenth century, following the deterioration of the centralised power of Serbia's Tsar Dusan. At the time, Montenegro was known as Zeta—a small region controlled by feudal lordships. The rugged mountainous terrain that covers most of Montenegro, leading down to the Adriatic coast, is dotted with small, fortified coastal towns. Although life in the mountains was very hard for the people of Montenegro, the terrain enabled its villages and towns to be well fortified from attacks by the Ottoman Turks and other invaders. Most of the old fortified cities overlooking the stunning Montenegran coast, along the Adriatic Sea, remain intact. Serbian Orthodox churches dating from the fourteenth century, built of durable white native stone, have been well preserved within coastal Montenegran towns.

Below: A Muslim woman and the debris of her home in Sarajevo after it was bombed in April 1995.

Left: *Another casualty of the civil war: St. Mary's Roman Catholic Church in Stup, Sarajevo, was nearly destroyed by shelling. A disconsolate parishioner surveys the wreckage.*

To the north of Montenegro is neighbouring Dalmatia—also known for its imposing old coastal fortress towns. During the Yugoslavian civil war of the 1990s, Montenegro was involved in military skirmishes centred between its northernmost coastal towns and Croatia's southern Dalmatian coast. Shelling occurred around the coastal cities of both sides, but luckily, there was only minor damage. Parts of the outer suburbs of Croatia's old fortress city of Dubrovnik experienced most of the damage, while the old city itself largely escaped destruction: there was minor damage to some of the stone walkways and rooftops.

However, cities and towns of Bosnia-Hercegovina were not as fortunate during the recent civil war. This region had always been a volatile cauldron of three competing Bosnian ethnic and religious groups: the Serbs, Muslims and Croats. The civil war that engulfed Bosnia-Hercegovina in 1992 resulted in the destruction of much of Sarajevo, Mostar and Banja Luka. This included houses, historic buildings and monuments, as well as places of worship in smaller towns throughout the countryside. It is estimated that hundreds of mosques, Serbian Orthodox churches and some Roman Catholic churches have been damaged or destroyed as a result of the civil war. The best-known casualty was the 500-year-old bridge over the Neretva River in Mostar, completely destroyed during fighting between Bosnian Croat and Bosnian Muslim forces.

Sarajevo, the capital of Bosnia-Hercegovina, experienced the greatest amount of damage during the 1992 civil war. The city was greatly expanded and built up after World War II, as were many other major cities in former Yugoslavia. Added to the charming old part of the city was the suburb of Grbavica—the new, developed area dominated by tall apartment buildings and industrial complexes. Since Grbavica's predominantly Serbian inhabitants fought a war with central Sarajevo's largely Muslim government, the destruction due to shelling occurred primarily within the city itself. As a result, there was major damage or destruction between 1992 and 1995, affecting hundreds of houses, apartment buildings, office buildings, schools, hospitals and the industrial sector of Sarajevo, as well as its mountainous suburbs.

Currently, the international community is working to provide financial assistance to areas of Bosnia-Hercegovina in order to rebuild the area's infrastructure and repair some of the historic and beautiful sites that have been damaged.

—Danielle Sremac

Aerial View of Ljubljana, Slovenia *Above*
The old city of Ljubljana, capital of Slovenia, is
noted for its historic architecture. Most of the
structures shown in this 1941 photograph still
remain, but the addition of new high-rise office and
apartment buildings has significantly altered the
skyline. Ljubljana's notable buildings include several
German Renaissance palaces, the Cathedral of
St. Nicholas, the Town Hall, dating from 1718,
and the national university.

Old Town, Dubrovnik, Croatia *Opposite*
A view of the Old Town, whose earliest buildings
were constructed of native stone during the seventh
century, when it was founded by Greek refugees from
Epidaurus. The city was a medieval centre of arts and
letters and is known as the cradle of Serbo-Croatian
literature. Aside from the recent civil war, Dubrovnik's
turbulent history encompasses centuries of conquests
by invaders including Arabs, Normans, Napoleon and
the Austro-Hungarians.

1930s View of Dubrovnik *Above*

Long known as one of Croatia's most beautiful and
interesting cities, Dubrovnik is the highlight of the
Dalmatian coast. Framed between the mountains and
the Adriatic Sea, its terracotta-roofed buildings,
monasteries and churches represent more than a
thousand years of history. George Bernard Shaw said
of it: "Those who seek paradise on Earth should come
to Dubrovnik." During the siege of 1991, over 2,000
shells fell on the city, causing damage to almost every
street. Restoration workers have already repaired much
of the damage sustained by the Old Town.

Dubrovnik's Citadel Walls *Opposite*

The city's walls and fortifications date from the
thirteenth and fourteenth centuries. Until its conquest
by Napoleon in 1808, it was a rich and powerful
republic and the only Dalmatian coastal town that was
never subdued by Venice. During the Middle Ages, its
commerce extended to the Hanseatic towns. Despite
bomb damage, the walls remain largely intact today.

City Hall, Sarajevo, Bosnia *Above*

This view of the City Hall and Miljacka River in
Sarajevo, the capital of Bosnia-Hercegovina, has been
drastically altered by the conflicts of this century. The
city was heavily damaged during World War II, in
which a million Serbs were killed and some 400
Serbian Orthodox churches destroyed. Extensive
rebuilding took place after the war, but much of this
effort was undone by the civil war, which brought even
greater destruction by prolonged shelling to hundreds
of the city's homes, churches, mosques, schools and
civic centres.

Spires of Sarajevo *Opposite*

Rising in an amphitheatre between river and hills,
Sarajevo has long been a colourful and cosmopolitan
city peopled by a variety of ethnic groups. At one time,
the city had both a Roman Catholic and an Orthodox
cathedral as well as a fifteenth-century Serbian
Orthodox church and a synagogue. The city's Oriental
character testifies to centuries of Turkish occupation
(1440–1878), during which many residents converted to
Islam, as seen by the graceful spires of the city's
mosques, one of them built by Hussef Bey in 1465. The
civil war has resulted in widespread damage to the
city's religious architecture.

The Stari Most Bridge, Mostar *Left and above*
At left, the historic bridge before its destruction by
Croatian shelling in 1993. It was a much-loved
landmark of this former capital of Hercegovina,
situated midway between Sarajevo and Dubrovnik.
With Sarajevo and Banja Luka, Mostar suffered the
greatest destruction during the recent civil war,
comprising houses, old fortifications originally built to
repel Turkish invaders, Serbian Orthodox churches
and mosques. Above, the remains of the stone
structure that survived centuries of earthquakes and
floods. A chain-link footbridge has been built to
provide passage over the Neretva. Destruction of the
old bridge ended a long history of the annual diving
contest among the local Muslims, Croats and Serbs—
a traditional rite of passage.

Romania

The traditional architecture of a nation is an intrinsic and vital element of her people's identity, history and culture. As historian Dinu Giurescu stated in his preservation report entitled *The Razing of Romania's Past* (1988), "Special care should be given to the present architectural fabric, which is a vivid testimony of history, a link between yesterday, today and tomorrow, a genuine component of the national heritage….A people without history, without a past, is like a boat without a helm plunging windward."

Romania, "Land of the Romans," is situated on the Black Sea, with Hungary and Serbia on her western border, Bulgaria to the south and Moldavia and the Ukraine to the north. The Carpathian Mountains and Transylvanian Alps divide the landscape, and the lower Danube River runs along the southern border and through the eastern plain. After Trajan's conquest in AD 106, the region was known as the province of Dacia; the Ottoman principalities of Walachia and Moldavia emerged during the fourteenth century, and Russian influence on the area grew in the late eighteenth century as the dominance of the Ottoman Empire waned. Modern-day Romania was christened in 1862, shortly after its formation through the union of Walachia and Moldavia (1859–61). A diverse society had evolved from the centuries-long coexistence of ethnic Romanians, Hungarians, Germans, Armenians, Serbs and Russians. Charles of Hohenzollern-Sigmaringen was elected prince by a plebiscite in 1866. He defended his young country in the War of Independence (1877–8) against the Ottoman Turks and, in 1881, he became Carol I upon declaring himself Romania's first king. Carol I's reign

lasted until 1914, when he was succeeded by his nephew Ferdinand. After World War I, Bukovina, Transylvania and Bessarabia were incorporated into Romania, creating her present-day boundaries.

Young Romania was largely rural—indeed, present-day Romania is less urbanised than most European countries, with approximately half the population living in rural areas and two-thirds of her land cultivated. Her urban architecture was diverse. Brasov, on the north side of the Transylvanian Alps, shows a strong German architectural influence, reflecting her ethnic history. Bucharest, the capital of Walachia from 1698, became Romania's capital in 1861. A French-inspired architectural style dominated as the city grew in the late nineteenth century, becoming known as "the Paris of the East." Many older dwellings were replaced with single-family brick houses in styles including Art Nouveau, Eclectic, Neoclassical, Neo-Gothic and Neo-Romanian, and the north-south and east-west boulevards were created. The vast majority of Romania's twentieth-century losses in terms of architectural heritage have been in and near Bucharest, which is featured in the photographs on the following pages.

The early 1900s saw construction of low-rise apartment buildings financed primarily by private capital and guided by city planning. This process gained momentum between 1919 and 1939, the period between World Wars I and II. The interwar years marked an era of distinctive cultural and historical progress in what is now regarded as traditional Romanian architecture. This legacy included houses built in varying styles, churches designed in a style based on the Byzantine tradition, resorts, water-

Opposite: Olari Church, in the suburbs of Bucharest, built in 1758 on Mosilor Avenue. "Traffic requirements" led to its removal to a new site, where it is dwarfed by a haphazard collection of taller buildings.

ing places and the street network that had evolved over the centuries.

Romania's Commission for Historic Monuments was founded in 1892. During the post-World War II years, the Scientific Commission for Museums, Historic and Art Monuments was established (1951), and the Commission for Historic Monuments was reconstituted as the Directorate for Historic Monuments in 1959. A listing of more than 4,300 cultural monuments was approved by the government in 1956. Architects, urban planners and cultural historians worked diligently in this cause until the precipitate dissolution of the directorate by the government in 1974. Since then, the manmade landscape, particularly that of Bucharest, has suffered devastation on a scale unprecedented in Europe.

December 1947 marked the end of the Romanian monarchy and the beginning of the Communist era. Gheorghe Gheorghiu-Dej became the Communist Party boss of Romania, which was then dominated by the USSR. Under Gheorghiu-Dej, rapid industrialisation began, prompting mass exodus from the countryside into the cities. Prior to this, some 80 percent of the peo-

ple had lived in villages with fewer than 1,000 inhabitants. In order to provide shelter for the recent arrivals, the Communist leadership initiated an extensive housing program. In 1964 Romania declared its political and economic independence from the USSR. The following year Nicolae Ceausescu succeeded Gheorghiu-Dej.

During the 1960s, issues like the increasing volume of traffic and the move toward universal availability of such amenities as modern plumbing and central heating were addressed throughout Europe. The concept of renovation of traditional housing was advocated by some; many more—on either side of the "iron curtain"— asserted that old cities, towns and street networks were unsuited to contemporary needs and that wholesale demolition and reconstruction of sections of these old towns was appropriate and desirable. Traditional architecture was destroyed in cities and towns of many countries in the 1960s and '70s as a result of this zeal for "progress."

As Ceausescu's plans for "modernising" Romania evolved, however, they reached far beyond the goals of updating industry and the national infrastructure, into the

realm of social engineering on a grandiose scale. Ceausescu introduced a programme of "systematisation," which involved the resettlement of villagers and peasants into urban areas and the construction of multi-storey apartment buildings to provide standardised housing. The changes were to be enforced "until the inhabitants [could be] persuaded of the great advantages offered:…schools, shops, running water, in short, good conditions of life." An official 1966 study in Romania concluded that renovation of existing sites was two to three times less expensive than demolition and reconstruction. Despite this, urban centres were targeted for wholesale razing and redevelopment, while the more efficient policy of combining urban preservation with construction of additional housing outside city perimeters was rejected. The political aim of systematisation, as expressed at successive Party conferences, was to homogenise society by the year 2000.

The 1974 Urban and Rural Systematisation Law laid the foundation for the radical new concept of "urban renewal." Its objectives, as reported by Giurescu, were: "the judicious organisation of the entire country's territory;…the determination of appropriate guidelines for construction density and height, for population density, for the creation of recreation areas and of technical and sanitary installations, of roads and transportation;…for increasing the efficiency of economic and social investments and of working and living standards of the entire population." In 1975 the Popular Council of the City of Bucharest announced its finding that only 7 percent of the structures built prior to 1943 were in good condition, while 61 percent of these buildings were substandard. Remodelling of the city centre must be undertaken: historical structures would be preserved only if they did not hamper "modernisation."

Demands for the protection of traditional Romanian architecture were stepped up as systematisation proceeded. Twenty-five historic centres had been identified for preservation and restoration by the Directorate for Historic Monuments. They included portions of Brasov, Sibiu, Sebes-Alba, Timisoara and Satu Mare. The government gave wide publicity to the restoration of such Bucharest buildings as the mansions on Ana Ipatescu Boulevard and the Central State Library and Tribunal, but almost all the nation's traditional architecture had been left in a state of decay, and the calls for conservation were silenced after the directorate was disbanded. The increasing decay and deterioration of "substandard" buildings was cited as the rationale for large-scale demolition.

In 1977 a natural disaster occurred: on March 4, a massive earthquake devastated many communities and left more than 1,500 dead. Bucharest experienced the greatest destruction. Since the city's older structures had suffered the most damage, while the newer buildings escaped relatively unscathed, the forces of modernisation gained support. The opportunity to implement widespread demolition had presented itself, and Ceausescu's régime seized it. The expression "in a state of imminent collapse" became the justification for the razing operations that followed the earthquake. It was also the rationale used to explain the fact that the Directorate for National Cultural Patrimony was not consulted about the demolition in Bucharest—a city widely regarded as among the most beautiful in Europe.

One of the first historic monuments to be demolished on Ceaucescu's orders in the aftermath of the earthquake was the Cerchez House in central Bucharest. Dating from the late nineteenth century, it was a fine example of the neo-Gothic style of the period, most recently used to house Romania's Union of Fine Arts. This demolition marked the beginning of a tragic phase in which traditional architecture in many towns, and more than fifty entire villages, would be completely and irrevocably lost.

To forestall objections from the Directorate for National Cultural Patrimony, the State Council issued decree number 442 on November 25, 1977, instituting the Council for Culture and Socialist Education. The

Directorate for National Cultural Patrimony and all of its restoration sites were disbanded immediately, to be replaced by the Central State Commission for National Patrimony, an organisation whose chief responsibility was "to implement the party and state policy by setting forth a national plan for territorial, urban and rural systematisation." The plan called for the accelerated implementation of the 1974 act, including the resettlement of the entire rural population (upward of 11,000,000 people) from traditional single-family houses to apartment buildings.

In May 1981 a new decree stated that all reusable materials and everything of historic, artistic, documentary, memorial or technical-scientific interest would be salvaged from all buildings that were to be demolished. The photographs depicting demolition of Bucharest's historic Vacaresti Monastery (1984–6) show that this decree was not always implemented. The frescoed interior, one of the major examples of iconographic Romanian art, was largely destroyed, and the intricate sculptured columns were piled with the rest of the rubble. As a material and spiritual entity, the Vacaresti Monastery was irreplaceable. Art historian Vasile Dragut had described it as "the most outstanding achievement of eighteenth-century Romanian architecture."

It is unclear how far the 1981 salvage decree was followed. However, during the 1980s, a number of listed historic monuments located in reconstruction sites were dismantled, moved and rebuilt or partially rebuilt at another site, rather than destroyed outright. In some cases, including the sixteenth-century Mihai Voda Monastery and the Olari church, both in Bucharest, buildings were moved only fifty to a few hundred yards. The Olari church was restored in its new location, but only the chapel and bell tower were "salvaged" (1985) from the Mihai Voda complex. These relocated buildings, including the Nun's Convent (partially restored) and St. Elia's Church, were often screened from view in their new locations by tall, new structures. The purpose of this kind of "salvaging" is difficult to determine; at any rate, the aesthetic and cultural significance of each of these monuments was either greatly diminished or destroyed in the process.

When news of the mass demolition that was occurring in Romania reached other countries, many took action to reinforce Romanian conservation appeals. Within Romania, despite the dangerous consequences of openly opposing Ceausescu's régime, conferences and symposia were held, letters were written to party heads and articles were composed for public distribution. The *Association internationale pour la protection des monumentes et des sites historiques en Romanie* was founded in Paris on March 1, 1985, to help enlist support for the defence of monuments and historic sites. Other countries that collaborated on preservation efforts included Belgium, Brazil, Canada, Italy, Spain, Switzerland, the United Kingdom and the United States. In 1987 an International Council on Monuments and Sites charter was signed in Washington, D.C., to which Romania was a signatory.

All appeals to halt the destruction went unheard, and the demolition continued. Charles Knevitt, architecture correspondent of the London *Times*, reported on February 9, 1988, that: "Local people [in Bucharest] refer to the destruction as 'Ceaushima,' a cynical reference to Hiroshima." One resident, who was quoted anonymously, lamented that: "They are trying to destroy our memories." Dr. Marcus Binney, president of Save Britain's Heritage, was quoted in the same article; he described the urban destruction as "the most systematic and serious blow to Europe's architectural heritage that has taken place since the Second World War."

Ceausescu's objective of "achieving a single society of the working people by accelerating the process of homogenisation" superseded any plans to conserve and protect Romania's architectural legacy. The cost

of the régime's brutal policy in human terms is harder to quantify, but the extent of the repression of individual freedom and choice went further than the forced evacuations. In effect, the very identity of the nation—and of each individual—was being steadily and inexorably undermined.

Ceausescu's destructive régime ended when he was forced from power on December 25, 1989; he and his wife were executed. The National Salvation Front assumed leadership under Ion Iliescu. An immediate halt to relocation of the peasantry and reconstruction of towns was announced, but real progress in rebuilding became possible only in November 1996, when sweeping economic reforms were instituted by newly elected president Emil Contantinescu.

One man's drive to bring Romania into his vision of a "modern world" had almost resulted in erasing her past. The beauty of Romania's architectural heritage had been fragmented more dramatically than that of any other country in twentieth-century Europe, despite the drastic effects across the continent of warfare, social change and industrialisation.

—Istvan Lazarescu

Below: The Eastern Orthodox St. Nicolae-Jitnita Church was built before 1590 and refurbished and extended by Captain Gheorghe Totoescu and his mother-in-law, Chita, between 1711 and 1718. Located on Bucharest's Nicolae Popescu-Jitnita Street, this sacred landmark was restored in 1851; however, it fell victim to "systematisation" during the summer of 1986.

Coltea Tower *Above*

Built between 1710 and 1715 by Mihai Cantacuzino on Coltea Lane in central Bucharest, the Coltea Tower was hailed as a symbol of the city as the Eiffel Tower is symbolic of Paris. When the mayor of Bucharest ordered its demolition in 1988, the area had to be permanently cordoned by the Communist police due to popular agitation. Today the foundations of this landmark lie buried under the tarmac of Bratianu Boulevard.

Sturdza Palace *Above*
Built in 1892, the ornate, eclectic Sturdza Palace was
demolished before the Communist régime took power
in 1947. The Romanian Foreign Office razed the
structure in 1938 in order to build new headquarters in
a modernist style on the site. The palace was designed
by Ion D. Berindei and financed by Dimitrie Sturdza,
who sold the palace to the Romanian Foreign Office
when he went bankrupt.

"Odeon" Music Shop *Above*
Located on Bratianu Boulevard, the "Odeon," with its
flamboyant Art Nouveau façade, was built by Leonida
Negrescu between 1910 and 1920. It was demolished
after the 1977 earthquake.

Brincovenesc Hospital *Below*

The Brincovenesc Hospital complex was built between 1881 and 1885 in the prevailing classical style for a charity organisation established by Princess Zoe Brancoveanu. The German architect Carol Benes was invited to settle in Romania by Prince Nicolae Bibescu Brancoveanu and became chief architect of Bucharest. Despite its status as part of Bucharest's historic central zone, demolition of the hospital began in December 1984.

Berzei Street *Above*

Between August and November, 1987, approximately 150 buildings were destroyed along Berzei, Stirbei Voda and Virgiliu Streets and the Calea Plevnei to enlarge Stirbei Voda and improve access to Ceausescu's palace. This late nineteenth-century eclectic residence at 37 Berzei Street was one of the buildings demolished. The only structures to escape destruction were a church, a school and four houses.

King Carol's Palace *Above*

The palace of Carol I, Romania's first king (1881–1914),
was partly destroyed by fire in 1930 and rebuilt as per
this period photograph, taken from the University of
Bucharest across the square. The elegant Neoclassic
building was most heavily damaged at the centre,
housing the rooms of state, and the right wing,
occupied by the king's Life Guards. The office building
at left, where the royal staff of secretaries worked,
sustained less damage. Buildings like these, identified
with Romania's royalist past, were the first targeted by
the Ceausescu régime for destruction.

Vacaresti Monastery *Below*

This Eastern Orthodox monastery, built 1716–22, was a symbol of Romanian history. It was founded by Nicolae Mavrocordat, ruling prince of Moldavia and Wallachia. Restoration of the property had begun in 1974, but the resulting improvements had been erased by 1986. Originally, it comprised a church, a bell tower, the royal residence, a chapel flanked by a two-storey gallery, the monks' cells, the abbot's residence, two kitchens and surrounding walls. The monastery was destroyed by the Romanian Communist Party Central Committee despite many pleas to stop the demolition that began in December 1984. Only a fraction of the monastery's famous fresco cycle was removed for conservation.

Russia

As Alexander Solzhenitsyn observed in his 1970 Nobel Prize acceptance speech, "The twentieth century is more cruel than the previous ones." It certainly has been more cruel to Russian architecture. William Brumfield, author of *Lost Russia*, hardly exaggerates when he characterises the twentieth century in Russia as "a cataclysm of rare proportions."

The upheavals of 1917 brought on massive destruction of cultural monuments, especially in the countryside, which was subjected to the kind of random violence and anarchy that the border states in America experienced during the Civil War. In addition to the destruction caused by the Red and White armies, violent mobs attacked and burned estate houses. When the Bolsheviks nationalised all property, paintings, statues, manuscripts and other valuable objects were taken to central deposit points—and then they vanished.

We will probably never know what happened to these treasures. Historians now estimate that there were tens of thousands of estates—some grand, some modest—scattered all over Russia in the nineteenth century; after 1945, perhaps as few as 500 remained. Priscilla Roosevelt, author of *Life on the Russian Country Estate*, considers it comparable to the loss that would occur if France's Loire Valley were to drop off the map one day.

By the late 1920s, Stalin had consolidated his power and used it to mount an extraordinary attack on the Russian Orthodox Church. He had priests imprisoned and shot without trial; churches were looted and turned into factories, warehouses, gymnasiums and offices. The Communists destroyed over 100 historically important churches in Moscow alone, and a comparable number in St. Petersburg, which had been renamed Leningrad. By 1939 the Russian Orthodox Church barely existed.

***Opposite:** Built in 1748–64 by Bartolomeo Rastrelli, the Resurrection (also known as Smolny) Cathedral, St. Petersburg, was a remarkable synthesis of Italian Baroque and Byzantine-influenced design.*

***Left:** Once described as a "paradise on Earth," the Liublino estate was built in 1801 and is attributed to Ivan Yegotov. Constructed in the shape of the cross of St. Anne, the estate contained its own theatre and theatre troupe. The influence of Renaissance Classicism is apparent.*

Above: Home of the Zinovyev family, this grand estate was one of the tens of thousands destroyed by the Bolsheviks in the early twentieth century.

Tver Street (called Gorky Street during the Soviet period) may serve as an example of the changes that Stalin visited upon Moscow in the 1930s. It begins at the Kremlin, leads to what was formerly the Square of the Passion, and then out of Moscow to the city of Tver.

The Kremlin was a more interesting and varied place before 1917. It featured impressive monuments to two Russian statesmen who fell victim to terrorists: Tsar Aleksandr II, murdered in 1881, and Grand Prince Sergey Aleksandrovich, assassinated in 1908. The Kremlin complex also included the Monastery of the Miracle, founded in 1365. Although this church was the site of many historic events, it was torn down in 1929, along with the adjacent Small Kremlin Palace. Two sixteenth-century churches, the Cathedral of the Saviour on the Pine Grove (now being rebuilt) and the Monastery of the Ascension, were also destroyed, in 1933 and 1929 respectively.

Stalin decided that he would make Tver Street the main street of Moscow. In the 1930s he implemented what might be called the "St. Petersburgification" of Moscow—the creation of bare, oppressive spaces for parades and other official functions. Buildings were lifted and rolled back or demolished. Many historical buildings were destroyed in the process; those that remained were often altered beyond recognition.

The Square of the Passion, which became Pushkin Square, has a most instructive history. The magnificent church of the Monastery of the Passion, which gave the square its name, dated from the seventeenth century. In 1880 a statue of Russia's national poet, Alexander Pushkin, was unveiled directly across from it. As part of the celebration of the centennial of Pushkin's death in 1937, the monastery and several nearby historical buildings were torn down, and the area was renamed Pushkin Square. Then, in 1950, Pushkin's statue was moved to the site of the monastery—an oddly appropriate move, because in the official absence of religion during the Soviet period, Pushkin became a kind of secular saint. Pushkin now confronts McDonald's—thereby creating a twentieth-century version of the opposition of the sacred and the profane.

The Nazi invasion of the Soviet Union on June 22, 1941, began a new round of destruction, both of human life and of cultural monuments. About 72,000 Soviet towns and villages were destroyed. The figures for southern Russia speak volumes: the fighting destroyed 90 percent of Stalingrad (now Volgograd) and Voronezh, and over 99 percent of Sevastopol.

During the Blockade of Leningrad (now St. Petersburg), the air raids caused great damage to the great city's many palaces, churches and monuments. However, the most infamous cases of damage occurred in and around Pushkin (formerly Tsarskoe Selo), the site of several eighteenth-century palace complexes that have extraordinary historical significance. Although these buildings had no military importance, the Nazis mined, exploded and shelled them. After the war, the Soviet government spent untold millions on the rebuilding and restoration of Petrodvorets and Pavlosk.

Both the Soviet government and its people had every reason to feel, and express, outrage at what the Nazis had done. But when the Soviet government denounced the Nazis for their dynamiting of the New Jerusalem monastery at Istra, it was

condemning the Nazis for doing exactly what it had been doing ever since 1917. This ambiguity may explain why Soviet prosecutors described in much more detail the damage to the estates of such artists as Leo Tolstoy, Alexander Pushkin and Peter Tchaikovsky.

Postwar reconstruction took its own toll of important buildings in Moscow, as Stalin decreed the construction of large apartment buildings, called Victory Houses, to form an impressive façade along the Moscow River. In the 1960s the creation of Kallinin Prospect (now the New Arbat), a straight street about a mile long and lined with modern office buildings, also entailed the demolition of many buildings in the Arbat area.

The collapse of the Soviet Union has given the Russian people new freedom, new excitement—and also a host of problems that the Communist régime had repressed. Moscow as well as such provincial cities as Yaroslavl are facing challenges unheard of ten years ago. Chief among these are automobile traffic in cities never designed for the automobile, and the management of urban growth in a way that respects the past while building for the future.

—JAMES CURTIS

Joseph-Volokolamsk Monastery, near Moscow Above
The photographs on these and the following two pages
illustrate the diversity of Russian church architecture,
which suffered huge losses through Communist
ideology, particularly in the 1920s and '30s, and was
further diminished during World War II. This
monastery was destroyed by the Germans in 1941.
The configuration of five domes is characteristic of
imperial Russian architecture, which had its roots in
fourth-century Constantinople, capital of the
Byzantine Empire until its conquest by the Ottoman
Turks in 1453.

Church Architecture in Novgorod Opposite
Novgorod is one of Russia's oldest cities, and her
magnificent and distinctive architectural heritage
includes many buildings from the eleventh to early
sixteenth centuries, despite severe losses during World
War II and an aggressive period of industrial growth in
the 1960s. The Cathedral of the Sign, opposite above,
dates from 1355, rebuilt 1688–89. It was looted and
damaged during World War II. Originally built in 1198
and rebuilt during the fourteenth century on the
inscribed Greek cross plan typical of the Orthodox
Church, the Church of the Transfiguration, opposite
below, was one of the city's most important churches.
Shown here after some damage to the western wing
and corner arches, the church was destroyed during
the war, and only fragments of Theophanes the Greek's
1199 cycle of interior frescoes survived.

Neoclassical Church Architecture *Above and right*
The Church of St. Nicholas and Bell Tower, right,
1774–76, by Ivan Starov, and the Cathedral of the
Monastery of Boris and Gleb in Torzhok, above, built
in 1785–96 by Nikolai Lvov, described by William
Brumfield as "one of the masterpieces of Russian
neoclassicism."

Simonov Monastery, Moscow *Opposite*
The "Muzzle Tower" and some of the original walls of
the medieval Simonov Monastery, one of several that
also served as fortresses on Moscow's border. During
the 1930s the building was altered for conversion into
an automobile factory, the ZIL (an acronym for
"Lenin Factory").

The Kremlin, Moscow *Above and left*
Moscow's Kremlin as seen from the Nicholas Palace before damage sustained during the Bolshevik Revolution, above, and the 1898 Monument to Alexander II, left. The statue, by Alexander Opekushin—better known for his Pushkin Square statue—was toppled in 1918, and the monument was destroyed in 1928.

Cathedral of Christ the Saviour, Moscow

Above and right

A Moscow landmark designed by Konstantin Ton and
dedicated in 1883 as a memorial to Russia's 1812 victory
over France, the monumental Cathedral of Christ the
Saviour was dynamited in June 1931 to make way for the
Palace of Soviets. A swimming pool, right, was created
in the foundation of the Cathedral when construction
of the Palace of the Soviets was abandoned due to
technical and financial problems. Reconstruction of the
Cathedral began in 1994 in the aftermath of the "new
revolution." As President Boris Yeltsin commented,
"This church shows Russia is alive."

Tver Street and Triumphal Arch, Moscow *These pages*
A 1928 photograph, above, showing the narrow Tver
Street before it was widened and partially destroyed
under Stalin's régime to create Gorky Street, one of
Moscow's central thoroughfares. The Triumphal Arch,
shown opposite in its original form, commemorated
the Russian victory over Napoleon in 1812. Located at
the beginning of Tver Street, the arch was dismantled
during the construction of Gorky Street and
reassembled, right, when the rebuilding of the area
was completed.

Cathedral of the Resurrection, New Jerusalem *Above*
An early twentieth-century view of the Cathedral of
the Resurrection (1658–85), which was part of a large
monastic complex at Istra known as New Jerusalem.
It was founded by Patriarch Nicon in 1658, and the
church was modelled on the Crusader Church of the
Holy Sepulchre at Jerusalem. Due to structural
problems, part of the roof collapsed in the eighteenth
century. The monastery was destroyed by the Nazis
during World War II.

Ruins of the Cathedral at New Jerusalem *Above*
Two women view the remains of the Cathedral of the
Resurrection, part of the complex also known as the
Voskrensky Monastery, after the German destruction.
The church's interior, rebuilt after the original dome
collapsed, was decorated by Bartolomeo Francesco
Rastrelli (1700–71), an Italian architect who is
considered the creator of the Russian rococo style.

Peterhof, St. Petersburg *Following page*
Peter the Great commissioned this celebrated palace
in 1715, intending to model it on Versailles. The steplike
structures carried a great cascade of water down to a
shallow pool. It was finished by Rastrelli during the
1740s for Empress Elizabeth. Most of Rastrelli's major
works, including the Summer Palace and the Smolny
Cathedral (see page 142), were in the St. Petersburg
area. Although it had no military significance, Peterhof
was almost completely destroyed during World War II,
as shown at top.

Pavlovsk, St. Petersburg Top
The palace complex of Pavlovsk (1782–6) was
commissioned by Catherine the Great for her son
Paul, and designed by Charles Cameron, an English
architect. Pavlovsk was destroyed during World War II,
but was later painstakingly rebuilt.

Prince Oldenburg's* Dacha, *St. Petersburg Above
One of the first structures on Stone Island, north of
the city, Prince Oldenburg's *dacha* (summer house)
was built in the 1830s. During the early twentieth
century, Stone Island was a fashionable area for
the Russian nobility.

Index

*Picture references appear in **boldface** type.*

Index

Acknowledgements

Lost Europe is a collaborative project that would not have been possible without the assistance and contributions of many. In addition to the contributors and project staff listed on the copyright page, the publisher would like to thank the following individuals in particular for their help in the preparation of this book: Carla van Splunteren, for translations; Nicola J. Gillies, for editorial assistance; Wendy J. Ciaccia, for graphic design; Frances Dorfman, Fred Gordon, Marc van Grieken, Terri Hardin, Clare Haworth-Maden, Karen Howard, John Kelly, Alain Lévy, Judith Millidge, Arkady Nebolsin and Chris Rundle, for additional research and advice.

Every effort has been made to acknowledge the copyright owners of the photographs, as listed below with the page numbers on which they appear; if any errors are found, the publisher apologises and will correct them in any future editions. The following institutions and individuals kindly gave permission for reproduction:
A.I.T., Tournai: 80t (F867-N33), 80b (F50-N19), 81t (F437-N10), 81b (F129-N10), 82t (F885-N8), 82b (F51-N49), 83t (F74-N28), 83b (F7-N9); **AFP/Corbis-Bettmann:** 129t; **AKG photo London:** 93, 100, 101; **Art Resource/Alinari:** 106, 109, 110, 111, 112, 113, 114t, 114–115b, 114t, 114–115b; 116; **Archives d'Architecture Moderne Bruxelles:** 76, 79; **Aurelian Stroe:** 132–33, 139l; **Bildarchiv Foto Marburg:** 96 (1-082-253); **Brighton Reference Library:** 39; **British Architectural Library, RIBA, London:** 26, 29, 35, 51t, 104t & b, 105; **Christian Bracacescu & Maria Uzoni:** 130, 135, 136, 137, 138, 139r, 141; **Clackmannan Local Studies Library:** 34; **Collection**

Gem. Archiefdienst Rotterdam: 70 (A-611625), 71 (G-2121), 74 (G-2865), 75 (1990-605-2); **Corbis-Bettmann:** 8, 42, 97, 118, 120, 125, 126, 128–29, 140; **E.A. van Blitz & Zoon/ Nico Jesse, Collection Municipal Archives Utrecht:** 60, 61; **Gemeentearchief Amsterdam:** 54 (D11585), 55 (D5464), 58 (10300-5Y), 59 (D4640), 72 (D19863), 73 (GM27-25); **Greater London Record Office:** 16 (A5568), 21 (77/8997), 22 (A5568), 23t (84/1680), 23b (2930), 24 (3674), 25 (67/07788), 27 (83/1941), 28 (58460), 38t (006046), 38b (66/07778); **Haags Gemeentearchief:** 67t & b, 68, 69; **Irish Architectural Archive:** 11, John Whybrow Ltd, Birmingham: 30, 31, 33; **KLM aerocarto luchtfotografie:** 66 (11063); **National Museum & Galleries on Merseyside:** 18–19 (SB-14051-2), 20 (SB-1613-282), 36 (SB-41339-1), 37 (SB-41206-1); **Novosti (London):** 146, 147t & b, 148, 152, 153t & b; **Peter Popken, Foto Dikken & Hulsinga, Leeuwarden:** 2–3, 57 (RB 34778/80102); **Reuters/Corbis-Bettmann:** 121; **Rheinisches Bildarchiv, Köln:** 92; © **Roger-Viollet, Paris:** 46b, 50–51bHarlingue-Viollet: 47t, 50t; LL-Viollet: 44; ND-Viollet: 40, 43, 45, 46t; **Sächsische Landesbibliothek:** 102t & b, 103t & b; **Saraband Image Library:** 62, 63; **Society for Cooperation in Russian and Soviet Studies, London:** 151t, 154, 155; **Underwood & Underwood/Corbis-Bettmann:** 10, 14, 32, 47b, 87, 95, 98t &b, 99, 124, 127, 142, 150t; **UPI/Corbis-Bettmann:** 122, 123; **Zaanstad Gemeentearchief:** 52, 64t, 64–65b; **Collection of Clara Brenger:** 84, 88, 89, 90, 91, 94t & b; **Collection of Jean Loussier:** 48, 49t & b; **Collection of Jim Curtis:** 143, 144, 145t & b, 149t & b, 150b, 151b, 156t & b, 157t & b; **Collection of Mila Riggio:** 108, 117.